P9-CRB-085

Praise for

"*Queer, There, and Everywhere* is so conversational, fast paced, and infused
with pop culture sensibilities that it tricks you into forgetting it's
a series of (incredibly timely) biographies. An absolute must-read for
people interested in their queer forebears, or for anyone who doesn't
already know the majesty of Elagabalus, empress of Rome."
—Meredith Russo, author of the Stonewall Award–winning *If I Was Your Girl*

"Accessible, irreverent, and meticulously researched, at times heartbreaking
and just as often wildly funny, this stunningly diverse survey of queer
histories is a nourishing and inspiring addition to our arsenal of queer
possibilities. Should be required reading for all of us, queer or not."
—Sarah McCarry, author of the Lambda Award–nominated *About a Girl*

"Recognition is so vital to who we are and who we are able to become.
Thank goodness we live in a time when queer kids can finally participate
in their history! *Queer, There, and Everywhere* is a valuable resource for all
those queer kids out there. Let them know they are not alone.
Let them know they have a history. This book is a lifeline and a gift."
—Justin Sayre, writer, performer, and author of *Husky*

"Wow. It isn't easy to tell stories from across time and space of lives we
would now call queer. Much less in an I-can't-put-this-book-down way.
Sarah Prager has done it, showing us all how to 'live bravely.'"
**—Leila J. Rupp, author of *Sapphistries: A Global History of Love between
Women*, coeditor of *Understanding and Teaching U.S. Lesbian, Gay, Bisexual,
and Transgender History*, and professor at UC Santa Barbara**

"Reading this book is like discussing history with a really good (and really
smart) friend—free of pretentiousness, full of wisdom, dispatched in a
casual but informative way. *Queer, There, and Everywhere* is a desperately
needed and absolutely brilliant breath of fresh air. A must-read!"
**—Shane Bitney Crone, activist and producer-subject of
the *Bridegroom* documentary**

"In *Queer, There and Everywhere*, Sarah Prager does the impossible: she takes several millennia worth of complicated history and makes it accessible and fun for young readers. Prager tells us twenty-two fascinating stories, some of them new twists on familiar ones (like Abraham Lincoln) as well as ones about figures who history has nearly forgotten (like the Roman emperor Elagabalus), mixing lighthearted humor with impeccable scholarship so that the reader keeps turning the page to see 'what's next.' In short, Prager combines fun and facts to present an unforgettable overview of two thousand years of queer history."

—Kevin Jennings, founder of GLSEN and former assistant deputy secretary of the US Department of Education, and author of *Becoming Visible: A Reader in Gay and Lesbian History for High School and College Students*

"*Queer, There, and Everywhere* is a powerful educational book about the lives of twenty-three LGBTQ people who made important contributions to our society. This is an essential tool to educate the world about our LGBTQ heroes and leaders."

—José Gutierrez, founder of the Latino GLBT History Project and cofounder of the Rainbow History Project

"In this delightful and accessible book, Prager introduces us to a wide and diverse assortment of twenty-three historical figures who challenged the gender and/or sexuality norms of their time and place and changed the world. I enjoyed every story."

—Robyn Ochs, educator and coeditor of *Getting Bi: Voices of Bisexuals around the World*

"This is a great book about some remarkable people who show us the actual diversity of real life. Gender isn't nearly as straightforward as most people pretend it is!"

—Dr. Susan Stryker, author of *Transgender History* and codirector of the Emmy-winning film *Screaming Queens: The Riot at Compton's Cafeteria*

QUEER, THERE, and EVERYWHERE

23 PEOPLE WHO CHANGED THE WORLD

QUEER, THERE, and EVERYWHERE

23 PEOPLE WHO CHANGED THE WORLD

By Sarah Prager

Illustrations by Zoë More O'Ferrall

HARPER
An Imprint of HarperCollinsPublishers

We gratefully acknowledge permission to reprint the poem
on page 45 from Inés de la Cruz, Sor Juana. *Sor Juana's Love Poems*.
Translated by Joan Larkin and Jaime Manrique. © 1997 by the Board
of Regents of the University of Wisconsin System. Reprinted by
permission of The University of Wisconsin Press.

Queer, There, and Everywhere: 23 People Who Changed the World
Text copyright © 2017 by Sarah Prager
Illustrations copyright © 2017 by Zoë More O'Ferrall
All rights reserved. Printed in the United States of America.
No part of this book may be used or reproduced in any manner
whatsoever without written permission except in the case of brief
quotations embodied in critical articles and reviews. For information
address HarperCollins Children's Books, a division of HarperCollins
Publishers, 195 Broadway, New York, NY 10007.
www.harpercollinschildrens.com

ISBN 978-0-06-247431-5

Typography by Torborg Davern
Art direction by Alison Klapthor
17 18 19 20 21   CG/LSCH   10 9 8 7 6 5 4 3 2 1
❖
First Edition

R0448501329

For Liz, and

all the queer activists making tomorrow's history

TABLE OF CONTENTS

INTRODUCTION

Quick question: Was George Washington straight?

Umm . . . yeah?

Most of us have probably never considered our first president's sexual identity beyond knowing that he was married to a woman. We just assume he was straight because history doesn't explicitly tell us otherwise. But when we make assumptions about any historical figure, we rewrite the past without even knowing it. What other assumptions are we making about the gender identities and sexualities of historical figures we *think* we know? And how do those assumptions shape the way we see the past—and our present?

The version of history we learn in school puts a straight, cisgender mask on almost everyone. But the truth is, queer people have been part of history throughout every era, on every continent. Being queer isn't new; queer people have existed for as long as *people* have existed! And acknowledging that fact does something major: it reminds those who identify as queer that they have proud queer ancestors who fought for their rights, that they have cultural grandparents who took a stand. No one is alone in being queer, and shedding light on past queer identities can help us dig for the whole story on any number of historical figures. Recognizing the world's rich history of queerness helps reduce homophobia, biphobia, and transphobia, and helps welcome queer identities to the mainstream with love and acceptance. That's important, not only for queer people but for anyone who feels left out of or incapable of relating to the popular version of history most of us know.

QUEER...

What do we mean when we say "queer"? The word means so many different things to different people, and its definition is changing all the time. For some, it's still a painful and derogatory term; for others, it's been reclaimed. For the purpose of this book, "queer" means anyone not totally straight or not totally cisgender—*anyone* outside society's gender and sexuality norms. "Queer" in this book does not only equal gay, lesbian, bisexual, or transgender (terms often lumped together in the abbreviation LGBT or GLBT). Those four words refer to specific modern identity labels, and only a few of them at that. "Queer" also includes labels like genderqueer, panromantic, and asexual, as well as identities of people who showed characteristics of queerness (like gender nonconforming or same-sex loving) before we had any labels for them. A lot of these words and constructions didn't even exist a couple hundred years ago. Seriously: the words "heterosexual" and "homosexual" weren't invented until 1869. But of course people of the same sex were into each other, dated, had sex with each other, and loved each other before the 1860s. They have done those things since forever. But putting present labels on past actions is tricky, which is why you need to choose your words wisely. (For more information about different queer terms, check out the glossary in the back of the book.)

So: the language we bring to the exploration of queer history is obviously as complex as the history itself. We're leaving out hundreds, if not thousands, of terms for different kinds of queerness just by focusing on the words we have in the English language. (For instance, around the globe there have been entire minilanguages used exclusively by queer people, like Polari in Britain and Gayle in South Africa.) In English, all language related to queerness was initially more focused on actual sex acts than on a sense of self. One early example is the word "sodomite," which means "a person who commits the crime of sodomy." "Sodomy" comes from the Bible, specifically the town of Sodom, which was synonymous with violence and cruelty, including, in one story, an instance of attempted same-sex rape. "Sodomy" was used to describe men having sex with men and then, natch, used to outlaw men having sex with men. Since self-identifying as "gay" wasn't yet a thing, it was *doing the sex act itself* rather than being homosexual that was illegal.

When a new sense of personal identity began to form around same-sex sexual attractions, language expanded accordingly. "Uranian" was used in 1800s Europe to mean "men with female spirits," and the word "bisexual" was also coined around the same time. (Previously, no English word had existed to describe a person sexually attracted to more than one gender!) Then, through most of the 1900s in Europe and North America, people with any kind of same-sex attraction were labeled "homosexual," without any room for identity complexity. Fast-forward to 1950s and 1960s North America, where there was a popular movement to adopt the term "homophiles" instead of "homosexuals," placing the emphasis on same-sex *love* instead of sex. Obviously, that didn't stick.

As for the ladies, we currently use "lesbian" to describe women attracted to other women. The term means "from Lesbos," the Greek island where the poet Sappho wrote about loving other women in the 600s BCE, though the word took on its current connotation centuries later. (Fun fact: The citizens of Lesbos, the original "Lesbians," unsuccessfully sued the Homosexual and Lesbian Community of Greece in 2008 for people to stop using that word to mean gay women.) "Tribade" (referring to "tribadism," an old word for scissoring) and "sapphist" (there's Sappho again) were used before "lesbian" was popularized.

And for the trans and gender nonconforming folks out there, Magnus Hirschfeld coined the term "transvestite" in 1910 (more on Magnus later). "Cross-dresser" was also common back then and was used more broadly than it is today. In the 1970s a bunch of words like transgenderal, transgenderous, and transgenderist were tried out before "transgender" was generally settled upon. One of the earliest words used to describe intersex people, "hermaphrodite" (now a slur but once the preferred term), came from the god Hermaphroditos, who in mythology blended with a nymph to become one being of two genders.

The language we use to describe people's identities matters; these words have a great deal of power. There are literally hundreds of ways to describe queerness in English alone— and it's important to respect the exact terms a person uses to self-identify. For gender pronouns in the chapters to come, we've made case-by-case decisions in an effort to respect how individuals described themselves; and you'll see in one story that we chose the gender-neutral "they" instead of "he" or "she." In a few stories we also used the birth name of a person who later transitioned to using another name; in modern times, it's almost always considered hurtful and rude to bring up a transgender person's birth name, and we only did it here either because that person used both names to describe themselves even after transitioning, or for historical clarity when unavoidable.

THERE . . .

There has been no time in human history when queer genders and sexualities didn't exist. From aboriginal Australia to Japanese folk culture to American slave plantations, people of all faiths, races, heritages, and cultures have been queer—every color of the rainbow and then some. Some of the individuals featured in the chapters ahead illustrate a few of the many different ways people have transgressed gender and sexuality norms throughout time. Others are historymakers you've heard of, but who you might not have realized had a queer side. And still others are the activists who shaped the queer rights movement that's ongoing today. Each one of them is a part of the story.

But before you get the lowdown on these twenty-three incredible individuals, it's important to have all the context.

What was going on around the world, and in their local communities, while each of them was alive? What strides had the queer rights movement already made? Global cultures have demonstrated various levels of queer acceptance—and intolerance—throughout history. For those cultures that did embrace diversity, tolerance became a lot harder when Christian European colonists conquered almost every corner of the globe in the fifteenth to twentieth centuries. Suddenly there was exactly one correct way to do gender and sex almost everywhere. Sure, some places maintained their unique structures, like the Bugis in Indonesia (who still have five genders instead of two), but the world overall had far fewer rainbow colors. A rise in the persecution of queer people can be linked to the rise of Christianity, though Christianity is certainly not the only religion to question the morality of queer identities and sexualities. The story of worldwide queerness is being written and rewritten across the globe every day, as mainstream attitudes change and understanding grows.

Europe

In ancient Greece and Rome, marriage between men and women was more about partnership and child-rearing than attraction or romantic love. It was normal for husbands to go to female concubines and/or to young boys to indulge their sexuality.

Queerness was also out in full view in the leaders of Al-Andalus, as Spain was called under Muslim rule in the 700s to 1000s. One of the male caliphs of Córdoba kept a male harem, and he made his wife dress as a boy and use the male name Djafar so that she could *ahem* excite him in the bedroom and ensure the continuation of the family line.

In the Middle Ages, "sodomites" were a popular scapegoat. If there was an earthquake or a plague or some other punishment thought to have been sent by God, one way to purge the town of evil was to round up some men who could be accused of having sex with other men and execute them. (Unfortunately, this scapegoating continues around the world today.) The Spanish Inquisition similarly targeted queer folk. European colonists exported homophobia everywhere they went, a legacy that still has a stronghold in many parts of the world. Most of the countries that outlaw homosexuality today do so because of prohibitions dating back to when they were British colonies, centuries before the UK became one of the world's most queer-accepting countries. Why homosexuals were one of the colonists' most popular scapegoats remains unclear. It wasn't just a bad interpretation of the Bible, since colonial states didn't outlaw greediness or other things Christianity forbids. Simply seeing homosexuality as "unnatural" likely played a major role; the colonists didn't recognize how ordinary it had always been in many cultures.

Queer Europeans didn't start formally organizing for their rights as a community until the very late 1800s, when queer advocacy first emerged in Germany. That's when they started thinking of themselves as queer people, instead of people who did queer things (like wearing clothes that didn't match the sex they were assigned at birth). Remember Magnus Hirschfeld? Well, he was a Jewish German doctor who founded the first queer rights group, pioneered sex reassignment surgeries, and led the first studies on same-sex attraction and gender nonconformance. Yay, Magnus! But then all that progress was pretty quickly undone when the Nazis came to power in the 1930s. Nazis arrested about a hundred thousand men for being homosexuals, sending many to their deaths in concentration camps. They also burned Magnus's Institute of Sexual Research to the ground. His foundation was resurrected later in the century, when Western European countries began making huge strides with queer-forward legislation. The Netherlands became the first country ever to legalize marriage equality in 2001. Yay, Netherlands!

Africa

Africa can be considered the world's most diverse continent in terms of race, culture, and language—and the diversity of queerness is just as impressive. Sex and marriage between males was common for the twentieth-century Zande of central Africa; people assigned male at birth took on female appearances and roles in the Mossi courts of Burkina Faso; women could become soldiers and take wives among the Dahomey (now in Benin); and the Ndongo (in today's Angola) had a leader, assigned female at birth, who ruled dressed as a man and had a harem of men who dressed as women, known as the leader's wives. Most of our sources documenting this precolonial African queer culture are from Europeans who wrote down their descriptions of these peoples when they first encountered them in the 1600s to 1800s. How long these gender nonconforming traditions had been going on before the Europeans' arrival is unknown.

The Europeans eventually succeeded in taking over much of the African continent and erasing many of the queer cultures that had been there. Not only did queerness become less accepted, but its history was repressed, and the mainstream narrative in much of twenty-first-century Africa has been that homosexuality is an import of the Western world. You can regularly see phrases like "homosexuality is un-African" on signs at antiqueer protests around the continent. And in 2009, a small group of American evangelicals traveled to Uganda and held a series of talks and workshops about the dangers of the "gay agenda" and the threat it posed to "traditional families." Later that year the Uganda Anti-Homosexuality Act was submitted to the parliament, which called for life imprisonment for "the offense of homosexuality" (same-sex sex or attempting to marry someone of the same sex); seven years in jail for an uncompleted attempt; and the *death penalty* for "aggravated homosexuality" (same-sex sex where one of the people is under age eighteen, is HIV-positive, or meets other special criteria). Straight allies weren't safe either: anyone who "aids, abets, counsels, or procures another to engage in an act of homosexuality" would be jailed for seven years. That means a mother who doesn't turn her gay son over to authorities is liable *to go to jail*. The version of this bill passed in 2014 had a maximum sentence of life imprisonment instead of execution for the "aggravated homosexuality" offense, but ten other countries in the world do still have death-penalty laws against homosexual acts, and more than half of African countries criminalize homosexuality.

But progress is being made. Despite police raids on queer bars and a constant threat of violence and murder, African queer activists are mobilizing in Uganda and elsewhere, holding Pride parades, circulating publications, and forming advocacy groups. No matter how many times the government and police try to keep them down, these brave activists keep going. And legal victories are beginning to pop up, with South Africa legalizing same-sex unions in 2006 and Mozambique decriminalizing homosexuality in 2015.

We know of intersex gods being worshiped in Hinduism as early as the first century—like Ardhanarishvara, who is split down the middle as half male and half female. Many of the famous male conquerors of the Middle East and Asia had male lovers, and it was pretty normal to be bi in their cultures.

Bisexuality and polyamory were the norm in Han Dynasty China too (we're talking BCE). Ten emperors in a row each had both a female wife and an official male companion. This practice came to an end when one emperor went overboard, showering his male partner with political promotions and luxury gifts; after the emperor died, government officials murdered the partner to prevent him from succeeding the throne as the late emperor had wished.

In South Asia, the *hijra* are people assigned male at birth and presenting as women; they are seen as nonbinary, neither male nor female. In India, Pakistan, and Bangladesh *hijra* are legally recognized as a third sex. The recorded history of a third sex and other transgender identities in this region dates back to the *Kama Sutra*, which is about two thousand years old. When the British ruled India from the mid-1800s to the mid-1900s, the *hijra* were outlawed as a "criminal tribe" and were strictly monitored and oppressed. Though there's still a lot of social stigma against the *hijra* in India, some are making huge progress: Laxmi Narayan Tripathi became the first trans person to represent all of Asia Pacific to the United Nations, in 2008, and Madhu Kinnar was elected mayor of her town in 2015.

Oceania

Did you know that queer people have their own country? The Gay and Lesbian Kingdom of the Coral Sea Islands. In 2004, a group of Australians protesting their country's refusal to recognize same-sex marriage declared themselves independent on a few sandy islands at the edge of the Great Barrier Reef. A gay man was declared emperor, and the country even has its own set of stamps featuring various queer pride symbols like the rainbow flag (which is, of course, the country's flag). Okay, it's uninhabited and not recognized by the United Nations, but it's still very much a thing.

As for the broader continent, there's evidence of several indigenous peoples of the Pacific Islands who counted male-male sex as an accepted part of their cultures in precolonial times. Today, your chance of landing on an Oceanic island where same-sex sex is legal is about fifty-fifty. But the cultures might be trending more toward equality: in New Zealand in

1999, Georgina Beyer became the world's first openly transgender member of parliament.

Latin America and the Caribbean

By now it should not be a surprise that, like everywhere else, Latin America has a rich queer history. Also not a surprise: colonialism was a huge setback and is still a negative influence today. Around half of Caribbean nations enforce antisodomy laws still on the books from when the British penal code was imported in the 1500s. Belize became the first country in this region to strike down the antiquated law in 2016.

Some of the indigenous peoples around Latin America were intolerant of homosexuality and gender nonconformity, while others were very accepting. Attitudes may have varied, but the arrival of Spaniards starting in the 1490s saw the mass slaughter of men across the region who seemed too feminine—an abomination, according to the new colonists.

Countries from Mexico to Argentina started organizing for queer rights as early as the 1970s. Five Latin American countries legalized same-sex marriage between 2010 and 2016. Still, most of the continent's nations don't have laws that allow transgender people to legally transition from one gender to another.

North America

Almost every Native nation across Canada and the United States (that's dozens and dozens of peoples) once honored Two-Spirit people—those revered and respected for having both male and female spirits inside them. Then—you guessed it!—along came colonists. The American colonies had early laws against sodomy, and the homophobia grew from there and ran rampant across the continent for centuries.

The United States really got their movement for queer legal rights going in the mid-1900s. That's when the first groups formed and the first demonstrations took place: everything from a 1965 sit-in at a Philadelphia restaurant to a 1966 riot at a diner in San Francisco. The national turning point is considered the 1969 Stonewall Riot in New York City (check out Sylvia Rivera's chapter for more on this), and nine years later in San Francisco the rainbow flag emerged as a queer symbol and spread from there.

Then on a July day in 1981, a *New York Times* headline read: "Rare Cancer Seen in 41 Homosexuals." The disease first became known as GRID (gay-related immune deficiency), and then as HIV (human immunodeficiency virus), the virus that causes AIDS (acquired immune deficiency syndrome). When it first took hold in San Francisco, no one knew what caused it, there was no test to find out if you had it, and there was no treatment if you did have it. It quickly spread worldwide through gay and bisexual men's circles. In the United States, 270,000 people had died of AIDS by 1994. Entire communities were lost; neighborhoods disappeared. The death toll was so high because the government and pharmaceutical companies didn't invest in treatment or prevention research. Activists made them pay attention with bold actions like "die-ins," unveiling a huge memorial quilt on the National Mall in Washington, DC, and putting a giant condom over one senator's house (yep). Today HIV remains a global pandemic that touches communities regardless of sexual orientation. Modern treatments mean that people who are HIV-positive can live long lives if they have access to medication; unfortunately, medication is very expensive for or unavailable to many.

The AIDS crisis of the eighties and nineties sparked a new wave of in-your-face activism across many countries, especially in the United States. Concern over the global crisis reignited the fires of queer activism that had begun in the fifties and sixties. Into the 1990s, 2000s, and 2010s, advocacy efforts burned brighter and brighter; advancements achieved during this era were, in a word, awesome. In the United States, we went from zero rights to . . . a lot more than zero. Although there is no federal antidiscrimination law to date, queer victories in areas like employment nondiscrimination legislation have been hard-won with many activists giving up their freedom, safety, and even their lives for the cause. The twenty-first century has built a mountain of rights and communities unparalleled at any point since the founding of this country. The time you're living in right now? Downright historic.

... AND EVERYWHERE

Queer history is world history: the stories of every culture from every era. It is sometimes a tragic tale of persecution, other times the heroic triumph of love and pride over discrimination. It is also the story of innovation—the discovery of new ways to be alive and be human, of new contributions to global societies. These are the stories waiting for you now. Prepare to see history in a whole new (rainbow) light.

ELAGABALUS
203–222

tl;dr The most scandalous teenage Roman emperor
you've never heard of

I t was your average day at the stadium—togas, Olympic-style games, a decent amount of day-drinking—and Zoticus, an accomplished athlete, was busy kicking ass in crowd favorites like sprinting and wrestling. Suddenly, midcompetition, he was snatched away from the games by a band of thugs who'd been sent by the palace. Turns out Zoticus was being summoned by the emperor, Elagabalus, who was always on the lookout for beautiful men. Zoticus was rumored to be *ahem* well-endowed, and the emperor wanted to meet him.

Upon arriving at the palace, Zoticus was adorned with garlands and immediately given a coveted position as a *cubicularius*—a kind of butler in the emperor's private quarters. When he was presented to the ruler who had beckoned him, Zoticus saluted: "My Lord Emperor, hail!"

Lengthening her neck in a feminine pose, Elagabalus shot a lustful look at Zoticus and said, "Call me not Lord, for I am a lady."

Keeping Up with the Emperor

Fourteen-year-old Elagabalus shocked Rome when she arrived from Syria, with her country's army at her back, to take the throne. Her power-hungry mother claimed Elagabalus had a right to rule as the illegitimate offspring of a previous emperor. But while Rome's teenage conqueror was very intent on ruling, she was equally intent on living as the woman she was on the inside—even though she had been raised as a boy. (While Elagabalus was not referred to with female pronouns in her time, we've decided to use them here because of evidence of her gender identity, such as calling herself a lady.) Despite her feminine dress and affectations, no one else saw Elagabalus as a woman, just a very eccentric, strange young man. Which was one of the main things the Roman government and public didn't respect about her. A man dressing as a woman? The male *emperor* dressing as a woman? Not. Acceptable.

It was bad enough that Elagabalus was a foreigner with strange traditions and gods, but it was even worse that she wasn't willing to conform to traditional Roman ways or beliefs. Her advisers had told her all along that it would be best to wear the typical male attire of a toga so she wouldn't shock her new subjects. Nope! Instead, before even arriving from Syria, Elagabalus had sent a huge portrait of herself in gaudy robes to hang in the senate so the public could get used to how she was going to dress. Her tastes were her tastes: while Roman clothing was made of plain wool, Elagabalus wore only the finest silk. Purple and gold robes accented by necklaces and bangles and nothing less than a glittering tiara on her head were her style.

It's no surprise that the new emperor soon had a reputation for extravagance. She hosted elaborate banquets, serving

QUEER, THERE, AND EVERYWHERE

delicacies like camel heels, peacock tongues, and flamingo brains. Even the dogs got goose livers. She had urinals made of onyx, canals filled with wine, and a gold statue of herself erected. The Romans had never seen an emperor like this before.

Real Housewife of Rome

Elagabalus married five women and two men (including Zoticus) during her almost four years as emperor. You read that right: *seven people in less than four years*. And that doesn't even begin to account for the number of affairs and hookups she had. And she was, if you forgot, a teenager while all this was happening.

Even though Elagabalus recognized herself as a woman, her marriages to men were considered same-sex. Rome had seen same-sex marriage before, even with former emperors, but it was far from common. And males sleeping with males and loving males was accepted, though by Elagabalus's time the practice was falling out of favor. But soon Christianity would rise as the dominant ideology, completely reversing Rome's tolerant stance on bisexuality.

Fortunately, Elagabalus didn't hold back an ounce of her fabulousness just because it wasn't popular. As Roman leaders, soldiers, and common people freaked out over her feminine ways, she kept on keepin' on as a normal Roman woman would: She plucked her facial hair, wore makeup, spoke in a high voice, wore women's clothing, and spun wool. She danced everywhere (while walking, while giving speeches, while performing animal sacrifices), not caring that dancing was frowned upon by the Roman elite. It's safe to say Elagabalus didn't really give a flying discus about pleasing the elite—or anyone else, for that matter.

The Bachelorette: Emperor Edition

The day Zoticus arrived at court, Elagabalus's lover at the time, Hierocles, found himself very jealous. So he slipped a drug into Zoticus's drink that rendered him *ahem ahem* unable to perform. Useless to Elagabalus in this state, Zoticus was stripped of his new honors almost as fast as they were given to him, and then he was thrown out of the palace. But the exile didn't last: eventually Elagabalus and Zoticus would marry in a public ceremony. Never mind that Elagabalus already called herself the wife of Hierocles, too!

Married or not, Elagabalus freely pursued the physical pleasure she wanted. She enjoyed setting up the palace to look like a brothel and playing the part of a concubine. She'd stand naked by the door, soliciting anyone who walked by. Some men who worked at the palace were instructed to take the bait and follow her into the bedroom as customers. As such, men were promoted within the court often based solely on their, um, *size*.

Elagabalus wanted to go a step further: she also offered a huge financial reward to any doctor who would give her surgery to create her own vagina. The Romans already thought it was weird she was circumcised, and rumors about other possible surgeries flew wildly—though she never actually had them. No doctor ever came forward with the solution she sought.

Plot Twist

Three years and nine months after Elagabalus had taken power at the age of fourteen, her own guards couldn't stand for all this scandal any longer. They turned on Elagabalus and killed her and those loyal to her, including Hierocles. The bodies of Elagabalus and her mother were dumped in a sewer that flowed to the Tiber River. A dazzling flame had been snuffed out for shining too brightly.

Elagabalus's short rule has largely been forgotten, in part because she hardly spent any time on actual politics and didn't leave a legacy of long-lasting reforms. But there's more to a reign than that: Elagabalus showed the Romans how fierce queerness could really be in the final years before Christianity took hold around the world. That's the queer spirit: live your life full out as *yourself*, no matter what others think.

JEANNE D'ARC

AKA JOAN OF ARC

1412–1431

tl;dr A cross-dressing teenager listens to the voices
in her head . . . and liberates France

The white light around Jeanne was blinding, and she knew the voices would soon follow.

These hushed voices had been coming to her ever since she was thirteen and just your average illiterate French peasant girl. The first time, she'd been terrified: it was a summer's day in her father's garden when all of a sudden the voice of Saint Michael boomed from somewhere off to Jeanne's right, telling her to lead a good life and that God would be with her. Now, after three years of similar saintly visitations, she wasn't so frightened anymore.

Except this time, the message was different. This time, as the voices began buzzing, the saints were giving her a mission she couldn't refuse.

Leaving Home

Jeanne was born and raised in the little town of Domrémy, an unremarkable farming community where life had been difficult because of the Hundred Years' War between England and France for the past, well, nearly hundred years. Besides farming, everyone's favorite hobby in Domrémy was being a devout Christian; Jeanne spent her weeks confessing and going to mass. And then, after she became a teenager, also tuning in to the voices that visited her. Sometimes it would be Saint Catherine, other times Saint Margaret, but they always came to her when she was alone. She began pulling back from her friends and spending more and more time at the secluded little chapel where she liked to pray and listen.

At sixteen, Jeanne was an old maid by fifteenth-century standards, and her parents soon arranged an engagement for her. Engagements back then were legal contracts, and your parents made it official on your behalf. But Jeanne wasn't having it. Inspired by the directives of the saints, she swore a vow of chastity and declared that marriage just wasn't for her. When word got out that Jeanne wasn't about to leap for joy down the aisle, the fiancé's family sued her family over breach of contract. That seemed like a good time to get out of town, and the voices had a plan for Jeanne to do just that.

For weeks, the voices had been telling Jeanne to go help the dauphin, the rightful heir to the throne, claim his title and be crowned King Charles VII of France so that the French could beat the English and finally be free from their rule. The voices had also been giving Jeanne some specific instructions to wear men's clothing while she did it. Yes, Jeanne claimed the Lord's saints told her to go against Deuteronomy 22:5, which says "a woman must not wear men's clothing, nor a man wear women's clothing, for the Lord your God detests anyone who does this." The voices didn't let up; they told Jeanne she must accomplish what they asked her to do, specifically to free the city of Orléans. So she ditched her skirt, put on men's clothes (not actually passing for a man), and set out with a band of six men (including her own personal chaplain) to tell Charles of her mission.

Mockingjay

When Jeanne arrived at the court at Chinon, Charles interrogated the inexperienced, cross-dressing teenager for three weeks and ultimately determined she had no ulterior motives. She was clearly fully committed to her cause and said she was just following orders . . . from a bunch of voices only she could hear. He figured he had nothing to lose by giving her a shot.

Jeanne's first test on the battlefield came at the city of Orléans, which had been under siege for six months. The English had taken control and the French people were suffering. But after a six-month stalemate that neither side could break, Jeanne liberated the city *in just four days*. How? Well, after the English laughed off Jeanne's warnings that she would attack and beat them if they didn't surrender, she ordered her troops into battle. For hours the French soldiers weren't able to make any progress. Then it got worse: as the sun began to sink, they saw Jeanne get hit with an arrow between her shoulder and neck. After watching their leader fall, the French prepared to call for retreat. Jeanne wouldn't let them. With the arrow still jutting from her body, she got up, held her flag high, and encouraged her troops to go on, and the French were finally able to overwhelm the English. But instead of rejoicing in her victory, Jeanne cried for the souls of all who were killed on both sides of the conflict. She'd never experienced anything like battle back in Domrémy and was forced to adjust quickly to life as a military leader.

News of this miracle traveled fast, inspiring the French people. Jeanne went on a winning streak, kicking the English out of France like nobody's business. After generations of war, the tide was turning. People cried just to catch a glimpse of her and be in her presence. Whenever Jeanne approached an occupied area, the English knew that when she gave them the option to surrender or be killed, it wasn't an empty threat. In town after town, the English waved the white flag without putting up a fight.

Winning on the battlefield was great, but *Jeanne's mission had always had two parts*, and now it was time to see Charles ascend to the throne. She and her army led the way to the city of Reims, where Charles would be crowned. At the coronation, Jeanne knelt before the new king, said "God's will is done," and wept.

With Jeanne's divine mission complete, the voices abruptly stopped. Only, she still wanted to keep going—on her own. Even without military support from Charles (or God), she kept trying to win back more land for France. It didn't go so well, and her winning streak soon ended. Charles didn't need her anymore. Her magnificent moment in the sun had passed. Now she was just a cross-dressing heretic starting fights she couldn't win. She was ultimately captured at Compiègne and sold to the English.

Girl on Fire

A year later Jeanne was put on trial at Rouen by a few dozen clerics for several crimes, including heresy and cross-dressing. She continued to wear men's clothing while imprisoned, which deeply disturbed her judges. Jeanne begged for permission to continue observing her faith, and was told she could attend mass as long as she wore women's clothes when she went. She said that just wasn't "in her."

After five months of a biased trial marked by endless questioning, serious illness, near starvation, and threats of rape and torture, Jeanne was sentenced to death. Despite staying strong and devout throughout her many ordeals, nineteen-year-old Jeanne finally broke. She desperately recanted everything and even signed a document saying the voices and all the rest had been a lie. She swore she'd never wear men's clothing again if only they showed her mercy. . . .

And they did: Jeanne was sentenced to life in prison instead of being burned at the stake. Later that day, she put on a dress for the first time in more than three years.

That's when the voices came back, and their message wasn't the revelation Jeanne had hoped for. She might have saved her own life, they told her, but Jeanne had damned her soul by disobeying their orders. She shouldn't have rebuked them.

When Jeanne's judges came to check on her a few days later, they were shocked to see her back in pants. Her guards had stolen her dress and wouldn't give it back—maybe as a kind of degradation, or a bad joke, or because they just really wanted her to be executed. If she didn't wish to be completely naked in front of these men, pants were her only option. She remained silent and steady when she was found guilty of being a relapsed heretic . . . right up until the moment when she called out for Jesus as she was burned to death at the stake (in a dress).

Sainte Jeanne

Jeanne's mother petitioned to have her daughter's name cleared, and twenty-five years later, a special retrial overturned the guilty verdict. Then, almost five hundred years later, in 1920, the pope made Jeanne a saint herself, patron of soldiers and France.

KRISTINA VASA

AKA CHRISTINA OF SWEDEN

1626–1689

tl;dr A gender nonconforming sovereign brings
peace and queerness to Sweden

Kristina slowed their horse from a high-speed gallop as they approached the Swedish border. There was no turning back now.

Dismounting, Kristina took off their dress and changed into men's clothing. They chopped off their hair to chin length and buckled on a sword. Kristina's temporary transformation to a male persona was now complete. From here on out, the name was Count Christoph von Donha.

Hours ago, Kristina had been the ruler of all of Sweden. Now, twenty-eight-year-old Christoph was about to stow away into Denmark anonymously.

"The Girl King"

A fast note on pronouns: "They" was not used during Kristina's time, but we've used this gender-neutral pronoun for Kristina because they were vocal about not feeling entirely female.

Kristina was a star at playing with gender from the moment of their birth. King Gustavus and his wife, Maria, were over-joyed when court astrologers predicted that pregnant Maria would give birth to a boy—an heir! And for several moments after Kristina entered the world, the baby's parents got to live out that fantasy: the nurses announced that a prince had been born.

But then the nurses took another look. The baby was hairy and loud (too hairy and loud to be a girl, they'd initially thought), but nonetheless it was a girl. Maria was crushed, while Gustavus smiled and said, "I hope this girl will be as good as a boy."

From the way the king raised Kristina, you'd think he never got the memo about not having a male heir. Kristina was just like the son Gustavus had always wanted: playing with toy soldiers instead of dolls, learning to hunt, wearing men's jackets over their dresses, swearing like a sailor, and sometimes pretending to twirl an invisible mustache. Walking by ladies in the palace, Kristina would bow and tip their hat as a man would do. Being royalty, they were never called out for being . . . eccentric.

But Kristina didn't have much time to enjoy a carefree childhood; Gustavus was killed in battle when Kristina was only six. At fourteen, Kristina started attending meetings of the Swedish leadership, and an adviser ruled as a placeholder until the young queen came of age at eighteen.

Kristina always had their nose stuck in a book and often studied just for fun. They got up before dawn to read before governing a country all day. Then, once they became queen, they prioritized science, literature, philosophy, and other lofty subjects in their court; Kristina bought entire libraries from other countries and held philosophical discussions every Thursday night. All this put Kristina on the map as one of the most educated "women" in the world during that time. Not to mention that they ended the Thirty Years' War—the very war their father had died in—and brought peace at long last.

All the while, Kristina refused to abide by gender norms, straddling male and female. Kristina once wrote:

> As a young girl, I had an overwhelming aversion to everything that women do and say. I couldn't bear their tight-fitting, fussy clothes. I took no care in my complexion or my figure or the rest of my appearance. I never wore a hat or a mask, and scarcely ever wore gloves. I despised everything belonging to my sex, hardly excluding modesty and propriety. I couldn't stand long dresses and I only wanted to wear short skirts. What's more, I was so hopeless at all the womanly crafts that no one could ever teach me anything about them.

Kristina even said in their memoir that women weren't worthy of ruling a country: "It is almost impossible that a woman should perform the duties required on the throne. The ignorance of women, their feebleness of mind, body, and understanding, makes them incapable of reigning." Yikes.

But Kristina certainly saw themself as capable, so were they the exception to the rule, or not a woman at all? There are many ways to answer that question. If Kristina had lived during our time, they might have identified as a transgender man, a cisgender woman, genderqueer, or something else altogether. They also may have been intersex. Since they lived in a time without our terms, there is no modern label to pin on them.

Courtship at Court

You'd think a superambitious and busy person like Kristina would've had no time for silly distractions like love or sex. And you would have been right—but then Ebba came along.

Ebba Sparre was a woman so beautiful, Kristina nicknamed her Belle. Rumors about their relationship circulated through the court's gossip mill. Kristina felt a "tenderness" toward Ebba that they didn't have for their other friends. The two often shared a bed (though this wasn't unusual for unmarried ladies of the time). Kristina once wrote to Ebba from abroad, declaring: "In whatever part of the world I may be, I shall never cease to think of you. . . . If I may never see you again I shall always love you. . . . While I live I will not cease to love you."

But we know rulers don't always get to choose who they end up with. Even if Ebba had been a man, she didn't have the right lineage or clout to merit a permanent place by Kristina's side. Kristina was trapped: queens must marry men—the *right* men.

Kristina didn't exclusively love women, but the queen did exclusively love their own independence. In the end only one man came close to winning their hand: their cousin, Charles Gustavus. Kristina cared deeply for Ebba and Charles (as well as one or two others) at different times throughout their life, but had more interest in romance than sex. Kristina once wrote to Charles: "My love is so strong that it can only be overcome by death, and if, which God forbid, you should die before me, my heart shall remain dead for every other, my mind and affection shall follow you to eternity, there to dwell with you." And the diet (the Swedish equivalent of congress or parliament) would've been perfectly happy with Charles as king. But Kristina said they "could not bear to be used by a man the way a peasant uses his field." And they certainly could not bear to be married.

"I Was Born Free and I Will Die Free"

Though Kristina declared over and over they would never marry, the diet simply wouldn't believe it. Convention dictated *she* would settle down when *she* found the right man. Kristina told the diet they would do no such thing, saying they "felt such a repulsion toward the marital state" that they "would rather choose death than a man."

Ultimately, Kristina made the impossible choice to give up

the throne. If they wouldn't marry, they couldn't be queen—
and they did NOT want to get married. The power, their father's
legacy, the entire 131-year-old royal House of Vasa: over. In the
end, Kristina made Charles king after all . . . just not as their
spouse. The diet begged, the country mourned, and Kristina
rejoiced. They were free.

Free! No more answering to others. No more compromis-
ing. No more pressure to marry. A blank canvas lay ahead,
and Kristina could paint it however they wanted. As they rode
across the border out of Sweden and into Denmark, they yelled
out, "I am free at last!"

Leaving Sweden Behind

Now, Kristina didn't ride off entirely alone. Ever the expert at
political negotiation, Kristina had secured themself a salary
for life, servants, and some land and power too. Not bad!

Kristina chose to settle in Rome, dropping the traveler dis-
guise and returning to their given name. They continued to
cheerfully disregard gender norms their entire life, wearing
both male and female clothing and romancing both men and
women. After giving up so much to be able to live the way they
chose, Kristina died peacefully after a full—and free—life.

JUANA INÉS DE LA CRUZ
1651–1695

tl;dr A Mexican nun falls for a powerful woman she can't have—then becomes a world-class poet and an advocate for education equality

*D*on't go, my darling, I don't want this to end yet.
This sweet fiction is all I have.
Hold me so I'll die happy,
thankful for your lies.

My breasts answer yours
magnet to magnet.
Why make love to me, then leave?
Why mock me?

Don't brag about your conquest—
I'm not your trophy.
Go ahead: reject these arms

that wrapped you in sumptuous silk.
Try to escape my arms, my breasts—
I'll keep you prisoner in my poem.

Prodigy

Juana Inés de Asbaje y Ramírez de Santillana, later known as
Sor Juana (that's Sister Juana in old Spanish), was seriously
gifted. All she ever wanted was to fill up her brain with knowledge, and then fill it up some more. Impoverished and the child
of a single mother, Sor Juana didn't have many opportunities

growing up in San Miguel Nepantla, a Mexican village nestled in the shadow of a volcano. She asked her mom if she could dress as a boy and sneak into college, but that was a big no-go. Sor Juana was destined to do what every other girl in New Spain (as Mexico was called then) was supposed to do: take care of the home and make a bunch of babies.

But Sor Juana wasn't having any of that. She taught herself to read and write capably by the age of six or seven. And because she felt like she wasn't learning fast enough, she cut her hair short—she felt a head shouldn't be "adorned with hair and naked of learning." Around age nine she moved to Mexico City to live with her rich aunt and uncle. Even with the step up in family wealth, she had no dowry and therefore couldn't marry any of the eligible men in the viceroy's court (he was the king of Spain's rep in New Spain, a kind of mini-king in his own right). Getting married was pretty much the Thing to Do for a girl of her time, so that presented a bit of a problem.

Sor Juana stayed dedicated to teaching herself everything she could from any source she could get her hands on, until she became literally one of the best educated women in New Spain. Word of this smart cookie quickly reached the ears of the very powerful viceroy, who decided to set up a test for Sor Juana to see if she really was all that. He gathered forty of the most educated men in the country to the palace: philosophers, scientists, mathematicians, poets. This group lobbed question after question at seventeen-year-old Sor Juana, trying in vain to stump her. No one could. Did she know this about geography? Could she recite that about literature? What about this in Latin? Yes, yes, and yes. Impressed, the viceroy decided to take Sor Juana under his wing and treated her as an ally for the rest of her life. But that didn't exactly solve all of our girl's problems.

A New Muse

Sor Juana did the only thing she could do, since marriage and education were off the table: she became a nun. Life at the convent of Santa Paula in the Order of San Jerónimo would allow her to keep studying without having to take care of a husband. The downside? Sor Juana was not allowed to leave the convent walls—ever. Her attendance at daily prayers was mandatory, which wouldn't have been a huge deal, except services were held at six a.m., nine a.m., twelve noon, three p.m., and seven p.m. (just in case you forgot for a whole three hours why you were there in the first place). The nuns spent the time between prayer services doing quiet activities like sharing meals and sewing. For Sor Juana, it was an opportunity for writing, having academic talks with visiting scholars, and playing word games.

It must have gotten pretty lonely in that convent, but one

of Sor Juana's most frequent visitors kept her busy. Maria Luisa Manrique de Lara y Gonzaga—aka the vice-queen, aka wife to Sor Juana's benefactor, the viceroy—became the subject of many of Sor Juana's more amorous poems. Maria Luisa came from an illustrious heritage of Spanish aristocracy and was drop-dead gorgeous (according to Sor Juana). "Loving you is a crime of which I shall never repent," Juana wrote. And in another poem: "That you're a woman far away is no hindrance to my love: for the soul, as you well know, distance and sex don't count." Line after line in poem after poem, Sor Juana poured out her heart about a love that could never be hers.

All that remains of this love are the poems and letters the two women exchanged—so besides knowing that Maria Luisa visited Sor Juana regularly at the convent, history doesn't reveal what may have happened behind cloistered walls. Notably, Maria Luisa did get Sor Juana's works published, canonizing her devotion for all of history.

Sor Juana went on to become one of the greatest poets ever to write in Spanish. She wrote poems and plays for the viceroy's court and they rewarded her convent with gifts.

Seems like all of this was a win-win, right? Not exactly. Writing about religion and love of God would be one thing, but Sor Juana wrote about *everything*, such as taking a stand for women's right to education, an incredibly bomb thing to do in seventeenth-century New Spain. Some members of the court weren't happy about Sor Juana doing all this secular writing. So, in response, Sor Juana published *The Reply of Sor Filotea*, a scathing letter to the archbishop that laid out all the reasons why women should be allowed to learn. She cited practicalities, like the way understanding chemistry would make women better cooks (ha!), and lauded examples of female intelligence like the previously mentioned kickass Kristina Vasa. She argued that access to knowledge should be determined by merit instead of sex, noting that some men "who merely by virtue of being men consider themselves sages" didn't deserve the privilege as much as some women. Get it, girl.

Even though she did a lot to advance feminism during her time, Sor Juana wasn't entirely certain of her own identity as a woman. She saw herself as somewhat genderless because she considered herself a virgin; for her, having sex with a man was what truly made you a woman. As for how she got away with openly declaring her love for Maria Luisa, it was excused as a poet's exaltation of royalty. Sor Juana's poems went beyond the average ode to the vice-queen's greatness, though, and she hints in one of her poems that "from all I did not say, [Maria Luisa] will sense the love beyond expression."

In the end, the writings Sor Juana left behind are her legacy. She died of disease in the convent in her forties, but her poetry lives on forever.

ABRAHAM LINCOLN
1809–1865

tl;dr A whole other side to the Great Emancipator

On a day two decades before Abraham Lincoln would vigorously call for unity in the Gettysburg Address, he was experiencing some very, very different feelings: "I am now the most miserable man living," he wrote in a letter.

In his thirty-one years of life, Abraham had never felt so heartbroken. Nothing mattered now that Joshua had left him, and he'd rather die than keep on living so miserably.

Abraham's friends came and cleared his home of razors and knives for his own safety, but they could only stand by and watch as he wasted away to little more than a skeleton. The once-vivacious lawyer barely had the strength to speak or get out of bed. The only thing keeping him from suicide was the feeling that he hadn't yet achieved something in his life that he would be remembered for.

The next seven months were more of the same, with Abraham living like a shell of his former self. But everything changed when he finally got what he'd been waiting for: a letter from Joshua, the person who meant most to him in the world.

Intimate Friends

Before Abraham met Joshua or became President Lincoln, he was brought up in a one-room log cabin in Kentucky. His family moved to Illinois when he was twenty-one, and Abraham worked as a shopkeeper, a postmaster, and a hired hand on a riverboat before being elected to the state legislature. Then, after passing the bar exam, he moved to Springfield, Illinois, in 1837 with the hope of starting his own law practice. He arrived in town on a borrowed horse with little to his name. First on the to-do list: find a place to live—and sleep. But when Abraham tried to buy a bed, shop owner Joshua Fry Speed told him it would cost seventeen dollars, a significant amount of cash for the time. Abraham didn't have the money and wasn't confident enough that he'd make it as a lawyer to let Joshua give it to him on credit. So Joshua made an offer that would change both their lives: "I have a large room with a double bed upstairs, which you are very welcome to share with me."

Real beds were a luxury item in frontier America, so it wasn't totally weird for two men to share one. But Abraham and Joshua didn't just spend a few nights or a few months sleeping together while Abraham got on his feet in Springfield; they made a home together for the next four years, even when neither of them had financial need for a bedmate. (Joshua literally sold beds for a living—there was certainly no shortage for him!)

According to Joshua, "no two men were ever more intimate," and Abraham's law partner said that the future president "loved this man [Joshua] more than anyone dead or living." Abraham and Joshua were "intimate friends," an antiquated relationship term that refers to an affection one step above a bromance. Before the words "gay," "bisexual," and "straight" existed, men were able to express their love for each other without having to prove whether their love was sexual or not. And in this case, there's no way to know for sure if Abraham and Joshua's love was or wasn't.

But men of their age were also expected to marry—marry women, that is—and Abraham and Joshua were both years past the usual age for getting hitched. They talked to each other all the time about being freaked out about the prospect of getting married. Abraham was flirting with the idea of proposing to his on-again, off-again girlfriend, Mary Todd, but wouldn't commit.

In the end, it was Joshua who took the plunge first.

Wedding Worries

Abraham's months of misery and suicidal urges began after Joshua left for Kentucky to find a wife. When he finally wrote Abraham that life-saving letter, it was an invitation to visit— an invitation Abraham jumped to accept. He bolted off to Kentucky to stay with Joshua, who nursed him back to health. Abraham even helped Joshua court his target, Fanny Henning, by distracting her overprotective uncle so the would-be couple could talk.

Once Abraham returned to Illinois (in considerably better shape than when he'd left), he and Joshua continued writing back and forth. They often wrote about that pesky issue of marriage, including Joshua's claim that his wedding night had been "indescribably horrible." Abraham was honest about being jealous of Josh's relationship with Fanny and worried that he'd be forgotten now that his friend was wed. But he also admitted being glad to hear that Joshua was "far happier than [Joshua had] ever expected to be." Months later Abraham asked Joshua if he actually *felt* happy as a married man and wasn't just happy that he'd made the choice to go through with it. Whatever Joshua said in his reply letter must have been reassuring, because days after receiving it, Abraham married Mary. Then again, one wedding guest said, "Lincoln looked and acted as if he was going to the slaughter."

Maybe Abraham had a touch of clairvoyance, because he and Mary were indeed miserable as a couple. He avoided spending time at home, and they fought whenever they were together. She threw anything in reach at him (potatoes, books, firewood, hot coffee) and once chased him out of the house with a knife. Though, they did manage to accomplish one of the main goals of marriage at the time: nine months after their wedding night, Mary gave birth to their first child.

The White House

Things between Mr. and Mrs. Lincoln weren't any better once they moved to Washington after Abraham won the presidency in 1860. Joshua and Abraham had drifted apart, and Abraham and Mary didn't even sleep in the same bed. Virginia Woodbury Fox, wife to the assistant secretary of the navy, kept a diary of all the hot DC gossip and confided in one entry: "Tish says, 'There is a Bucktail soldier here devoted to the president, drives with him, and when Mrs. L. is not home, sleeps with him.' What stuff!" The president had found someone else to warm his sheets: David Derickson.

David, with his intense eyes and dark-black beard, was a career military man. Rugged-looking, David was a member of the Bucktail Brigade from Pennsylvania, so nicknamed for the fur they wore on their hats. One day the president asked David to ride with him on his commute to the White House from his summer cottage, and they were inseparable for the next four months. Fellow soldier and historian Thomas Chamberlin wrote about David that: "In Mrs. Lincoln's absence he frequently spent the night at [Abraham's] cottage, sleeping in the same bed with him, and—it is said—making use of his Excellency's night-shirt! Thus began an intimacy which continued until the following spring." Abraham and David did everything together for a while, from attending church to touring battlefields.

But no one ever compared to Joshua.

Surprisingly, it was the Civil War that eventually brought the two back together. Joshua was a slave owner and had disagreed politically with the president on this issue for a long time. But after years of chilly silence between them, Joshua dropped everything and hightailed it from Kentucky to Washington to assist the North's cause, even though he was against the abolition of slavery. He helped General Sherman secure resources for the Union directly from the White House—putting him in Abraham's path once again. The president's secretaries commented that "Speed and Lincoln poured their souls out to each other" throughout the war.

Another Kind of Love

Joshua and David both lived on with their wives after President Lincoln's assassination. Abraham had never done much to hide who he spent his time with, either because he didn't care or because people didn't suspect there was anything going on between him and these men—or because intimate male friendships were just accepted back then. It really was a whole different world when it came to same-sex relationships just a couple hundred years ago; sex between men was more hated and outlawed, but a certain shared intimacy was just fine—even for the president.

ALBERT CASHIER
1843–1915

tl;dr A transgender soldier keeps his identity a
secret throughout the Civil War

With their siege against Vicksburg, Mississippi, the Union soldiers were hoping to take down the last Confederate stronghold on the Mississippi River. But for one Union soldier, Private Albert Cashier, things were not going as planned.

. . . Okay, more like they were a major disaster: Albert had been captured by a Confederate soldier while staking out Vicksburg and was being held by enemy forces. Fearless as always, Albert wanted more than anything to get back in the fight.

In a moment of quick thinking, Albert grabbed a musket from one of his guards and used the butt of it to knock the man down. He made a run for it and managed to find his way back to his unit . . . but not to safety. Albert had left safety behind many years ago—along with his assigned female identity.

America

Albert's life had never exactly been what you'd call safe and secure. He grew up in Ireland during the Great Potato Famine and, like many of his fellow countrymen, had always planned to escape to the land of opportunity. Ships bound for America left frequently, and all Albert had to do was walk from his small town to the nearest harbor a few miles away. Getting on a ship was no guarantee you'd make it to America, though, and sinking into the Atlantic or dying on board of disease were so common that the vessels carrying would-be immigrants were called "coffin ships."

Then there was still another hitch: Albert wasn't yet "Albert"; he'd been raised as Jennie Hodgers.

When the day finally arrived to board a ship bound for America, Jennie decided to ditch the skirt and petticoats on the way to the harbor, start using the name Albert D. J. Cashier, and live as a man from then on. Whether Jennie chose to take on this identity in that moment or had been thinking about it for a while is anyone's guess. Lots of women passed as men during this era for all kinds of reasons, like safety while traveling alone. But most women didn't then continue to live as men. Albert was different; his transformation ran deeper than mere convenience, and he stayed in his assumed identity for more than fifty years. Though the word "transgender" didn't yet exist, Albert clearly felt that his true gender didn't match what everyone assumed it was. Leaving Ireland was the perfect chance to start living life as the man he was.

At the port, Albert discovered the price of a ticket: the equivalent of three hundred dollars today. Coming up with that much was about as likely as an iPhone falling from the sky in the 1850s. He decided he would sneak aboard and stow away.

Albert pretended to bid a sad good-bye to a group of people standing on the dock (P.S.: they were actually complete strangers), then walked boldly onto the ship like he belonged there—though he didn't have a ticket. His bravado did the trick, and the two-month journey passed without incident. Albert arrived in Boston a new man. Literally.

"A Right Feisty Little Bastard"

The streets in America weren't exactly paved with gold, as the rumors in Ireland had claimed. There was no work, which meant no money, which meant no food. Plus there was that whole living-as-a-man-for-the-first-time thing on top of it all. So Albert started making his way west, working odd jobs as a handyman along the way. He settled in Illinois, but not for long, since an opportunity as close to golden as he'd heard in his nineteen years presented itself seemingly out of the blue: a steady job with food and clothing provided. On August 3, 1862, Albert D. J. Cashier enlisted in the army. The medical exam was a joke; the Union was desperate for soldiers, so Albert had no problem getting in and never had to show more than his hands and feet to be admitted. He was the smallest in his company, and his comrades-in-arms teased him about it on the reg—but they had no reason to suspect he'd been assigned female at birth.

Albert had no problem keeping up with the other men in

Company G of the Ninety-Fifth Illinois Volunteer Infantry, not even when they marched from Illinois to Kentucky to Tennessee to Mississippi to Louisiana to Alabama (ten thousand miles in three years!). Albert largely kept to himself, but whenever he did interact with the other soldiers, they loved him. While he was shy and private around camp, he was battle thirsty. He'd taunt Confederate soldiers into the open so he could shoot at them, and everyone wanted to be by his side during missions. A fellow soldier remembered: "He was a right feisty little bastard. Sooner fight than eat!"

One day, the troop's flagpole broke, sending the Union colors into the dirt. Albert ran out through heavy fire, picked up the flag, climbed a tree with it, and waved it back and forth for all to see. His captain tried to scold him for taking such a risk, but Albert shot back, "Those colors should be flying free!" Later, his sergeant commented, "He might be the littlest Yankee in the company, but by golly, he sure carries his share of the fight!"

Miraculously, while many others died in battle and of disease, Albert made it through three years of war unscathed. An injury would have led to the discovery of his secret, but his assigned-female body was never revealed. Conveniently, soldiers rarely changed in front of each other and always slept in their baggy uniforms, which didn't show much of a body's shape. He was just one of the guys—albeit one who didn't grow any facial hair.

A Life in Illinois

After the war, Albert settled down in Belvidere, Illinois, working again as a handyman and then as a farmhand. He wore his military uniform every day, probably because he couldn't afford to buy any other clothes. Out of battle, he went back to being his shy-but-charming self. Each night he'd light the kerosene streetlamps in town, then pass by later to put them all out. It was a quiet life, especially compared to his time in the war.

Things took a turn for the worse one day when Albert was working as a mechanic. His employer, not very skilled at maneuvering newfangled contraptions called automobiles, ran over Albert's leg with a car.

After all those years, a doctor finally discovered Albert's secret.

But in an age when the word "transgender" didn't exist, those who knew Albert accepted him as the man they knew he was. His employer, the doctor, and others who helped care for Albert while he healed kept what they knew about his body to themselves. Still, Albert's health declined. After a few months it became clear he needed more help than they could give, and Albert was admitted to the Soldiers' and Sailors' Home.

Albert was checked in as Jennie Hodgers, but the small group of staff who tended to his baths guarded the secret.

Albert was able to live as a man at the home, receiving visits from fellow veterans to reminisce about war stories. And he still wore his uniform every day.

Respect at the End

As Albert's health deteriorated, at the age of seventy he was transferred to a less accepting institution: the women's ward at a psychiatric institution. They forced him to wear a dress, against his protests. Walking with a skirt around his feet was foreign to him, and he tripped over it one day, falling hard and hurting his hip. He was bedridden after that and never recovered.

After such a horrible turn of events at the end of such an extraordinary life, something wonderful happened. At Albert's funeral, soldier after soldier from the Ninety-Fifth came forward to make sure he was buried as the man he'd lived as—the man he was. The town of Belvidere welcomed him back, and Albert was given a full military burial in his uniform with an American flag over his casket. And the name Albert Cashier was engraved on his headstone.

GERTRUDE "MA" RAINEY
1886–1939

tl;dr The sexually empowered Mother of the Blues
blazes a trail for future VMA winners

The women in the room were buck naked. Every last one of them.

When the Chicago police received the noise complaint and drove over to Ma's apartment, they hadn't expected . . . well, *this*: women, *all* women, all completely naked, scrambling for their clothes. They were making a run for it, disappearing into the night. An arrest for a female orgy wouldn't be good on anyone's record—especially in 1925.

Many of the ladies, grasping at garments, made it out the back door before the police could arrest them. Ma wasn't so lucky. She was caught after falling down the stairs, and she proceeded to spend the night in jail. But Ma would have even further to fall—and higher to climb—before long.

Mother of the Blues

Way before Ma was hosting orgies, she was developing an ear for music. She learned to sing from her grandmother, who'd been a stage performer after being freed from slavery on a Southern plantation. Ma, born Gertrude Pridgett in Columbus, Georgia, first heard the blues at a traveling tent show when she was a teenager. She was instantly hooked and joined a minstrel show later that year. While minstrel shows did rely on dehumanizing racist stereotypes, through them, Ma and other black performers were able to make their own living and travel around the country. "Touring with the band" might not seem like much of a bold move now, but in Ma's time, the echoes of slavery still reverberated loudly through America's culture, and seemingly simple acts of freedom were a huge deal.

Ma was a natural performer and quickly gained popularity on the traveling musician circuit. She soon met William "Pa" Rainey, a seasoned performer who turned his charm way, way up on Ma. It wasn't long before Gertrude became "Ma" to William's "Pa," and they made it big as Rainey and Rainey, Assassinators of the Blues. They even had their own furnished train, today's equivalent of a private G6.

Like so many showmances, Ma and Pa's relationship couldn't stand the test of time. A dozen years after they got together, Ma left Pa—both their musical act and their marriage. She hadn't hesitated to sleep with other men and women while she was married, but now she was really free.

Ma had always been able to fill a room when she entered it, and her popularity quickly exploded as a solo act. You could always hear her coming as she made her way to the stage, her heavy jewelry jangling. This short, round black woman glittered gold from her teeth to her signature gold-coin necklace. And up on stage, the sequins from her dress and headband would shimmer in the lantern light.

Back then, no blues songs had ever been formally recorded and few people outside the South had even heard of the blues. Traveling performers like Ma made the rounds in former slave states, playing segregated shows (white on the left, black on the right) where "colored" audience members spent a good share of what they had earned in fields or factories that week on a ticket. They wanted to hear about the struggles they knew too well, and if they wanted original music about real life, Ma's show was the place to go.

Ma was singing about physical labor, inequality, grief, cheating, and domestic violence at a time when most mainstream music was about perfect hetero relationships and how pretty the moon was. Ma was Beyoncé singing about black lives mattering while other pop stars are writing songs about the dance floor—tackling raw, human issues from the stage even when her peers were playing it safe. Her songs weren't only about the struggle of being black in America; she was also among the first to sing about women having their own sexual desire. The women in Ma's songs didn't see marriage to men as a given: she sang about having a husband and a lover at the same time, and how she'd take any man who could pay her bills. Female musicians who top the Billboard charts now, singing about having sex and liking it, owe a serious debt to Ma Rainey.

Prove It

Ma was bailed out of jail the morning after being arrested for hosting her "indecent party"—the only orgy of Ma's to make the record books (though of course there could have been others). Since the police hadn't actually *seen* any sex acts taking place, just the nudity, they couldn't charge her with anything else. The arrest could easily have been career ending (around the same time the publisher of *The Well of Loneliness*, the first modern lesbian novel, was on trial for obscenity). But instead of sweeping the incident under the rug, Ma played it up by releasing the song "Prove It on Me Blues." Her record label's newspaper ad for the single showed Ma in a men's suit flirting with two flapper women. Scandalous!

> *Went out last night with a crowd of my friends*
> *They must've been women, 'cause I don't like no men*
> *It's true I wear a collar and tie . . .*
> *Talk to the gals just like any old man . . .*
> *They say I do it, ain't nobody caught me*
> *Sure got to prove it on me*

After ten more years of incredible success, Ma eventually retired from a music industry hit hard by the Great Depression. Popular music was moving on from her "down-home" style as jazz gained momentum. After Ma passed away a few years later, a fellow female blues singer sang, "People it sure look lonesome since Ma Rainey's been gone."

Ma's personality and energy made her famous, and in some ways those characteristics have endured more than her music. There was just something about Ma that couldn't be captured or contained—and it's that special something we see echoed in the music of modern female artists who might not even know how bravely Ma Rainey blazed the trail before them.

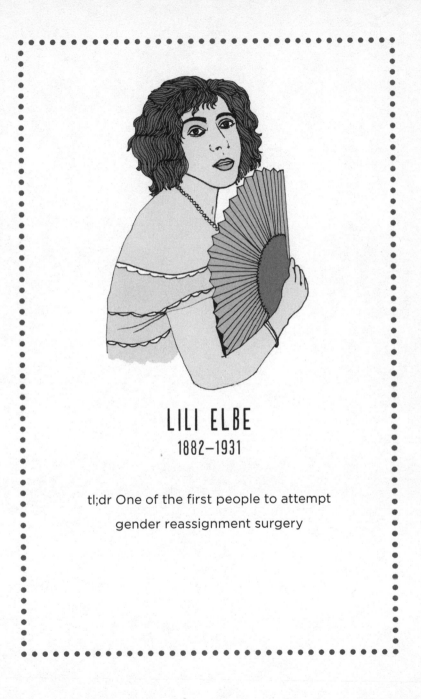

LILI ELBE
1882–1931

tl;dr One of the first people to attempt
gender reassignment surgery

F amed Danish painter Einar Wegener couldn't stop looking at his reflection in the mirror. To his surprise and delight, a beautiful woman stared back. The dress and stockings he wore felt beyond natural, as if he'd been wearing women's clothes his whole life. Einar's wife, Gerda—also a painter—stood by squealing with joy at her husband's newfound beauty.

Gerda's subject for a portrait had been running late that day, so she'd asked Einar to briefly model for her so she could paint the draping of the dress around the subject's legs and high-heeled feet. Einar refused at first, but after some begging, Gerda got her way. Even though she only needed to paint the legs, Gerda had had fun putting a wig and makeup on her husband in addition to the heels. Now, stepping back to admire her work, she said, "You look just as if you had never worn anything but women's clothes in your life."

The actual model arrived soon after and was equally overjoyed by what she saw, saying to Einar: "You were certainly a girl in a former existence, or else Nature has made a mistake with you this time." She even stopped Einar when he went to change out of the clothes, saying she couldn't bear to see him as a man again after witnessing the fabulous woman he'd become. She also suggested a new name for his feminine alter ego: Lili.

The name—and the identity that went with it—stuck.

Lili Is Born(ish)

Lili might not have been physically born that day, but her spirit certainly was. And until Lili's physical transition about twenty years later, the male Einar and female Lili would share a body. Einar didn't feel like a woman trapped in the wrong body; he felt as if a woman completely separate from him had been *born into* his body and that woman didn't want to share.

Einar was happily married to Gerda, who proved herself Einar's perfect partner in the truest sense of the word, encouraging Lili's full emergence after that day in their studio. The couple had fun "creating" Lili and playing dress-up, but Einar's cross-dressing and alter ego quickly became much more than that. Lili took on a life of her own; before Einar knew it, he was spending more and more nights as Lili, dressed in his wife's clothing.

Eventually Einar and Gerda realized that only Einar or Lili would survive. They couldn't share one body and one mind; they were completely different people and neither could live half a life. Lili and Einar each spent time being suppressed, wishing they could have their own body and life. Einar loved and hated Lili at the same time. He truly cared for her and wished she could be let out, but he also recognized that his life as he knew it would cease to exist if she were.

Decision and Transition

In the 1920s there weren't any resources out there for transgender people—at least not any accessible ones. Einar couldn't just Google "gender dysphoria" and find a Tumblr community devoted to positive messaging about what he was experiencing. That very same German doctor who coined the term "transvestite," Magnus Hirschfeld, had also coined the term "transsexualismus" in 1923 and created the first clinic for sex and gender transitions in Berlin. But Einar didn't know about Dr. Hirschfeld; instead, he went to regular doctors, who told him he was completely insane. They said there was nothing they could do for someone so "disturbed" besides lock him up in an asylum.

Einar made a decision: he would kill himself on May 1, 1930, just a few months away. He felt better knowing an end to the torment was in sight, because living this double life had indeed become a kind of torture. Lili was desperately trying to be her own woman, and Einar didn't want to stand in her way any longer. Einar was ready to give up even if it meant Lili would also die with him.

Thankfully, in February 1930 Einar met Dr. Kurt Warnekros. Kurt was different. He understood Einar immediately. Einar wept with relief as Kurt told him that he likely had underdeveloped ovaries in addition to his external male genitalia (which turned out to be true, making him intersex) and that he could help. "I understand you. I know how much you have suffered." More beautiful words were never spoken. Lili might survive after all!

Lili Is Really Born

Physical transition would entail a series of dangerous, mostly experimental procedures beginning with eliminating the original external sex organs and ending with adding internal ones. Einar's first surgery—castration—was a success. Incredibly painful to recover from, but a success. A couple months later, Einar underwent two more surgeries to get a vagina and fully developed ovaries. Gerda was there to hold Lili's hand as she recovered. The clinic where the operation was performed was located by the River Elbe in Dresden, Germany; Lili would consider this her birthplace, and the month of the surgery— April—her birthday. Einar was gone by May first, just as he had planned.

Lili was like a brand-new child. She didn't see herself as ever having lived in Einar's body and didn't see his experiences and memories as her own. She was a new person, part of the world for the first time. Even her handwriting was different. Only Gerda remained a consistent part of her life after she left Einar behind. They went out shopping for dresses together, arms linked like affectionate sisters. Besides Gerda, Lili had almost no one to rely on.

Sometimes Lili felt like she had murdered Einar, and she felt guilty for taking the place of a talented artist. She wasn't a painter and would never try to be. Many of Einar's friends didn't warm to Lili; they just couldn't wrap their heads around what had happened.

Gerda and Lili found themselves in a unique situation. While their bond was intense, they certainly weren't husband and wife (and "wife and wife" was hardly an option, because one, same-sex marriage was not a thing in Denmark yet, and two, both women only were interested in relationships with men). The king of Denmark granted a special decree making Einar and Gerda's 1904 marriage null and void, since technically the man who married Gerda no longer existed. The divorce became official on October 6, 1930. It was one of the first times a government gave legal recognition to someone like Lili as the woman she was. She also received a Danish passport recognizing her as a female with the name Lili.

Meanwhile, people started to wonder what had happened to the famous painter Einar Wegener. So Lili and Gerda decided to go public. A newspaper article was published explaining the transition and announcing Lili Elbe. The news was received relatively well. The Danish people were a little scandalized, but they didn't label Lili's transition as sick or wrong. Crowds flocked to buy Einar's paintings, allowing Lili to live off the income.

Trying for Another New Beginning

Gerda remarried in 1931, and Lili was overjoyed when an old friend, Claude Lejeune, proposed to her. But something held her back from saying "I do." She had only been alive for fourteen months and there was one thing that still felt unfinished: getting a uterus so that she could give birth.

Lili returned to Dresden for that final surgery, so excited about life afterward and the possibility of having a baby. But she died three months later of complications from rejecting the new organ. She had written to a friend from the clinic before her final surgical procedure: "It may be said that fourteen months is not much, but they seem to me like a whole and happy human life. . . . If sooner or later I should succumb physically, I am quite reconciled. I shall at least have known what it is to live."

FRIDA KAHLO
1907–1954

tl;dr A bisexual Mexican woman paints her pain and
has the world's most famous unibrow

On a Thursday after school, two teenagers in Mexico City were sitting together at the back of a bus. Frida had always told her parents that Alejandro was just a friend, even though they'd been a couple for a while. (And, actually, they were on their way to his house to hook up like they did most afternoons.) Carefree and in love, neither had any idea that life for one of them was about to change forever.

The streetcar careened toward them out of nowhere, and the bus split into a thousand pieces on impact. People and splinters of wood sailed through the air. A passenger's pouch of gilding powder—finely powdered gold used to make paint—exploded, sending the gold dust flying; the hazy afternoon sparkled.

When Alejandro, mostly unharmed, got out from under the rubble, he found Frida in the debris. She was naked, her clothes having been torn off by shrapnel. And her body . . . well, it wasn't at all the same as when Alejandro had last seen it: the angles looked painful, and she was covered in blood that glittered gold.

Still, it was going to be all right. At least all her limbs were intact, and she was conscious, and she was breathing.

Then Alejandro saw that part of the debris wasn't just lying on top of her, it was going straight through her.

An iron handrail from the streetcar had pierced Frida's body from one side to the other. Entering her back, it had exited through her vagina. When a fellow survivor wrenched the bar out of her, Frida's screams were louder than the sirens of the incoming ambulances. Later, she would say this was how she lost her virginity.

Recovery

Frida (well, Magdalena Carmen Frieda Kahlo y Calderón . . . Frida for short) hadn't been a typical high schooler before the accident in 1925. Her friends had been a group of mostly boys who hung out talking about philosophy and revolution. They devoured books and pulled off legendary stunts, like the time they set off a small bomb next to one of their teachers during class to protest his refusal to teach them about Marx.

The short-haired girl didn't care that it wasn't ladylike to run and play sports. And she didn't care that she embarrassed her parents, even once showing up to a family portrait dressed in a man's suit. She also didn't mind the limp that polio had left her with. Frida was content to march to the beat of her own drum.

Everything changed after the accident.

While eighteen-year-old Frida's spine, ribs, pelvis, right leg, and collarbone were all fractured in multiple places, she had survived. But in the years to come, she would often wish she hadn't. She spent a month in the hospital lying on her back in a full-body cast, mostly alone and completely immobile.

Frida underwent thirty-six surgeries in her remaining twenty-nine years of life. She suffered daily pain as each fragmented bone and shredded organ tried to stitch itself back together. And though her pelvic area healed, she was told she couldn't have kids. Her spine was never the same, and as an adult she had to wear metal corsets to keep her upright.

Back at home after her hospital stay, Frida stared at the wall, stared at the ceiling, stared at Alejandro's back as he left forever. And so Frida began painting out of sheer boredom. Well, boredom and necessity, given that her arms and hands were some of the only body parts she could use. It was no surprise that her subject was the person she spent the most time with: herself. She fastened a mirror to the top of her canopy bed so she could look up at her model and complete dozens of self-portraits.

Three years after the accident, when she was healed and able to walk again, Frida lugged her paintings through the streets to someone she thought could give her some artistic direction: the world-famous Mexican painter Diego Rivera. Diego was as well known for sleeping with his girlfriends, lovers, and wife as he was for his politically motivated art.

Diego was creating a mural in the middle of Mexico City when Frida called him down from the scaffolding. "I didn't come here for fun," she said. "I have to work to earn my liveli-hood. I have done some paintings, which I want you to look over professionally. I want an absolutely straightforward opin-ion, because I cannot afford to go on just to appease my vanity." He told her honestly that her paintings were good enough to make herself a career. Diego later said of that moment they met: "I did not know it then, but Frida had already become the most important fact in my life."

The Other Accident

Frida said that she had two accidents in her life: the bus and Diego Rivera. Both Frida and Diego quickly forgot that one of the first things she ever told him was "I have not come to flirt." Moving fast for 1920s Mexico, they shared their first kiss a few days after they met.

Frida wasn't the typical fangirl flitting in and out of Diego's life, and he knew it. When he began to court her, her parents were relieved that someone who could afford her medical bills had taken an interest (even though he wasn't exactly their ideal son-in-law). Despite Diego's being twice Frida's age and having a well-earned reputation as a "woman chaser," her father seemed more concerned for the muralist than for his daughter:

"I see you're interested in my daughter, eh?"

"Yes."

"She is a devil."

"I know it."

"Well, I've warned you."

When they married a year later, Diego was a three-hundred-pound forty-two-year-old and Frida was a ninety-eight-pound twenty-two-year-old. People said it was a union between "an elephant and a dove."

And boy, were the elephant and the dove dramatic together. They didn't set out to have an open marriage, but they did each hit the double digits in the number of people they slept with while married. And every new fight outdid the last. She would throw a vase against a wall, he would slash a painting with a knife, and they would both yell as loud as they could. They lived separately in side-by-side houses connected by a bridge, but Diego often found the entrance to Frida's on the other side locked.

Just when Frida thought she could handle his casual dalliances with models, she discovered his long-term affair with her own younger sister. This time, it felt as if the streetcar's handrail had stabbed her through the heart. She was so used to pain—both physical and emotional—that she buried the feelings of betrayal and continued on as a better wife than ever. She put Diego's career first, bringing him lunch each day while he worked on one commission or another. She traveled with him for months through the United States as he painted murals, even though she hated "Gringolandia" and sorely missed her beloved Mexico.

Halfway through their twenty-five years together, they divorced for one year. But eventually they were drawn back to the marriage, to each other. Frida and Diego were opposing magnets that always ended up passionately joined no matter the force of the resistance.

Her Own Mistresses

Frida's affairs with men made Diego wildly jealous, but he didn't seem to mind her liaisons with women. Her life's motto was "Make love, take a bath, make love again." Everything from lying still to having sex brought more pain, but Frida wanted pleasure too, and she didn't stop pursuing it.

Frida reportedly bedded prominent artists like American painter Georgia O'Keeffe, Mexican actress Dolores del Río, American-born French performer Josephine Baker, Hungarian photographer Nickolas Muray, Mexican singer Chavela Vargas, French painter Jacqueline Lamba, and American artist Isamu Noguchi. She even slept with the American actress Paulette Goddard—after Paulette had had an affair with Diego.

And through it all she painted. She painted the pain of her body and of her marriage to the elephant. The public began to see her as the painter Frida Kahlo instead of the wife of Diego Rivera. The surrealists of Paris thought she was one of them, but she insisted that she painted her reality (her world was just surreal to outside observers).

Twenty-nine years after the bus accident, Frida's health began fading more rapidly. She had lost a leg and a few toes in some of the thirty-six surgeries she'd endured, and she was once again bed bound. Her marriage with Diego was as calm and happy as it had ever been, and this time he took care of her instead of the other way around.

Though her work already hung in the Louvre, Frida was particularly determined to attend the first exhibition of her own paintings in her home country of Mexico. Her doctor had ordered her to stay in bed, but Frida had never been one for following rules. She decided to bend them instead of breaking them this time: she had herself delivered *in* her four-poster canopy bed to the gallery as a piece of performance art. It was the final show of her life.

MERCEDES DE ACOSTA
1893–1968

tl;dr A magnetic writer sleeps her way through
Old Hollywood's A-list

Rafael couldn't throw a ball as well as the other boys, and their taunts about him throwing like a girl stung like needles. The tension among the group was growing and the New York City playground was starting to feel like a battle-field. Eventually, Rafael challenged the leader of the half-pint group to a fight.

Instead of putting up his fists, the boy dropped his pants and showed Rafael his penis. "Have you got *this*?" he asked.

Rafael was horrified at the sight of something so . . . strange. "You're deformed!" Rafael said.

"If you're a boy and you haven't got *this*," the boy taunted, still holding his junk, "then *you're* the one who's deformed." Other boys pulled out theirs as further proof that a penis wasn't an abnormality.

Seven-year-old Rafael ran home to his mom and demanded answers. That's when Mrs. de Acosta looked her child in the eye and admitted the truth: Rafael had been born a girl—a girl named Mercedes.

"Who of Us Is Only One Sex?"

For the rest of her life, Mercedes referred to that day as "the tragedy."

"In that one brief second everything in my young soul turned monstrous and terrible and dark," she wrote. Mercedes had lived happily and naturally as a boy until that moment, thanks in large part to her mother. Mrs. de Acosta noticed that her child, assigned female at birth, was demonstrating a lot of masculine qualities in her youth and just sort of . . . went with it. She cut Mercedes's hair short and encouraged her to play boy games. Mercedes thought of herself as a boy right up until she found out that the other boys had penises . . . and Mercedes didn't.

After "the tragedy," Mercedes's parents, immigrants from Cuba and Spain, got spooked. They started looking into studies about the perversion of "masculine women" and came upon the story of a lesbian teenager from Tennessee who murdered her girlfriend because she wouldn't marry her. That story, and other negative messages about lesbians, made the de Acostas think their daughter's extreme tomboy tendencies might be a bigger problem. Her parents did a one-eighty and sent her to a convent to learn how to be feminine.

Mercedes told a nun at the convent, "I am not a boy and I am not a girl, or maybe I am both—I don't know. And because I don't know, I will never fit in anywhere and I will be lonely all my life." After what Mercedes had just been through over her gender identity, it's no wonder she had such a depressing outlook on life.

Mercedes didn't get why everyone was so hung up on genitalia when it came to gender. Mercedes might have fit right in with the nonbinary crowd today, but this was a hundred years ago, when male/female constructions were even more rigid. As an adult she later wrote: "I do not understand the difference between a man and a woman, and believing only in the eternal value of love, I cannot understand these so-called 'normal' people who believe that a man should love only a woman, and a woman love only a man. If this were so, then it disregards completely the spirit, the personality, and the mind, and stresses the importance of the physical body."

Mercedes seems to have chosen to identify as a woman, but neither did she deny her masculinity, once writing, "Who of us is only one sex?" She dressed like a mod pirate, with silver-buckled shoes, long capes, and a signature tricorn hat, all in black and white only. All she was missing was a sword as she strode down New York City's wide avenues. Mercedes wrote for a living—mostly plays and poems. But she isn't remembered as much for that today. Mercedes's prowess with the ladies, and her brazen openness about it, is what really cemented her reputation.

A Casanova

Truman Capote explained it best when he said that Mercedes de Acosta was the most valuable card to have when playing the game he called "international daisy chain," where you try to connect one person to another through everyone they've slept with. With Mercedes in the mix, he said you could get from a cardinal to a duchess.

Women didn't stand a chance when they encountered Mercedes, who left a trail of broken hearts in her wake. Champagne and caviar were part of her MO in wooing the objects of her affection. The women she seduced were always famous and intriguing, like dancer Isadora Duncan, who wrote a steamy poem praising Mercedes's naked body, and movie star Ona Munson, famous for her role as Belle Watling in 1939's *Gone with the Wind*. Ona once wrote a letter to Mercedes saying she wanted to "pour my love into you." Mercedes wasn't kidding when she bragged, "I can get any woman from any man." Mercedes even helped start the trend of women wearing pants by sending her female lovers to her tailor for custom pairs. One time a paparazzo snapped a buzzworthy shot of one of Mercedes's famous lovers leaving the shop, and when pics of the celeb were published, everyone wanted to look like her.

Even on the crowded roster of Mercedes's A-list lovers, the famous actress Marlene Dietrich stood out. Like most of the women before her, Marlene became almost obsessed with Mercedes. After the two met, the actress showered Mercedes with flower deliveries. Tulips, roses, and carnations kept arriving at Mercedes's home, sometimes twice a day. More than one hundred rare orchids were once flown in from San Francisco. "I was walking on flowers, falling on flowers, and sleeping on flowers," Mercedes remembered. She told Marlene to quit it and donated all the flowers to a local hospital. Marlene didn't take the hint and started delivering nonfloral gifts instead: vases, scarves, lamps, pajamas, and just about everything else you can imagine. Mercedes returned them all. The pair ended up laughing about it and starting a nine-month affair.

Marlene didn't tone down the enthusiasm, though. The gifts continued: cakes, handkerchiefs, hair products, buttons, watches. She also wrote Mercedes letters even though they saw each other almost every day. She even tried to encourage a relationship between her daughter and Mercedes—she was *that* sure they would be in love forever. Mercedes knew they wouldn't, but while it lasted she called Marlene her "Golden One." She probably loved Marlene's statement that "in Europe it doesn't matter if you're a man or a woman. We make love with anyone we find attractive."

Oh, and did we mention that Mercedes was married to a man for most of this? No? Well, she was. For fifteen years, starting in 1920, Mercedes was married to the painter Abram Poole, though she refused to go by "Mrs." All of Mercedes's sisters had married, and her mother was putting on some pressure, so she agreed to the marriage on the condition that she would keep her last name. Mercedes and Abram were friends and lovers until the couple split up when Mercedes recommended Abram take a model he was fond of as his mistress. She meant it as an innocent suggestion because she was worried about him being lonely, but he was offended. Abram divorced Mercedes and, not for nothing, married the model. Mercedes thought it was ridiculous to end a marriage over something as silly as sleeping with other people.

The Leading Lady

All these relationships were meaningless flings compared to the one woman who dominated Mercedes's life: Greta Garbo. Greta was the one who had Mercedes wrapped around her finger instead of the other way around. No matter what relationship either was in at the time, for decades Greta could beckon and Mercedes would come running.

They met in 1931 at a party in Hollywood, where Mercedes had just arrived to work on a screenplay. Greta complimented Mercedes on her bracelet and Mercedes took it off and gave it to her, saying, "I bought it for you in Berlin." Mercedes didn't know it then, but she would be hooked on Greta for the next thirty years.

Greta Garbo was from Sweden and had a reputation of being as cold as her homeland. Her public persona was serious, and she stayed as private as possible. She had only been in the United States a few years when Mercedes came into her life; she helped the actress improve her English and manners, since she was from a wealthy family. Mercedes helped her career in other ways too, like adding lines to the movie *Queen Christina* (yes, Greta wore men's clothes and kissed a woman while playing our dear Kristina in a 1933 film!). Mercedes got to see a warmer side of the Nordic actress for a while, but eventually the icy wind turned against her.

Greta was furious when Mercedes published her tell-all autobiography in 1960. Mercedes violated the actress's years of careful privacy because she needed the money. Now it was Mercedes who sent mountains of gifts in desperation. In the winter of 1961, Mercedes sent a Christmas tree that Greta never acknowledged. Mercedes took it as a good sign that she didn't send it back, so she followed up with a gift basket. Greta returned almost all of it, keeping just the bottle of vodka.

The next years were a painful downward slope for the writer, due to a series of debilitating health problems. When a friend told Greta she should visit Mercedes and get some closure before it was too late, she responded that she had enough on her plate. Mercedes died of natural causes without seeing Greta again. In her last poem to her beloved, Mercedes wrote, "You and me. There is no other way."

ELEANOR ROOSEVELT
1884–1962

tl;dr So much more than FDR's first lady

T he inauguration might as well have been Eleanor's sentencing.

She sat numbly behind her husband as he droned on, captivating all one hundred thousand people in the audience— everyone except her. Out of boredom she focused her attention on the sapphire-and-diamond ring on her left hand. It had been a gift from Hick, a reminder that someone loved her. Even if that someone wasn't her husband.

Hick . . .

Eleanor wished it was yesterday evening again, when she and Hick were together in Eleanor's bedroom reading over a draft of Franklin's inaugural speech. Now that Eleanor was first lady, it would be much harder to find the time and privacy to be together . . . but maybe if they could figure out a way to steal more nights like last night, the loneliness would be easier to bear.

"The only thing we have to fear is," Franklin intoned from behind that giant podium, "fear itself."

Eleanor sure knew something about overcoming fear. After all, it was the 1930s and her beloved Hick was a woman.

A Changing Partnership

Everything changed fifteen years before the inauguration, when Eleanor found the letters.

They were from Lucy Mercer, Eleanor's secretary . . . and they were addressed to Franklin. What the letters revealed was a less than *professional* relationship between Lucy and Franklin—a relationship that had apparently been going on for two years.

With her typical stoicism, Eleanor offered her husband an out: divorce. But at a time when only 1 percent of marriages ended, their elite families and political advisers reminded them that splitting up would mean Franklin getting fired from his high-up job in the navy, as well as an end to his political career. His mother threatened to cut him off financially if he left Eleanor for Lucy, not to mention that there were their five kids to think about. So Franklin promised he'd never see Lucy again—which turned out to be just one of many promises he wouldn't keep.

Even though Eleanor stayed in the marriage, the sexual part of their relationship was closed for business. Eleanor thought of sex as an "ordeal to be borne," anyway; she didn't feel particularly maternal, feminine, or even sexual, and decided she no longer needed to play the role of a typical wife. It was as if she'd been living on autopilot since the moment her uncle Ted (US president at the time, Theodore Roosevelt) had walked her down the aisle to marry her distant cousin Franklin when she was twenty. Discovering the affair with Lucy finally snapped Eleanor awake; she felt free from her obligations to Franklin and his political aspirations, and she was determined to pursue her own interests.

At the time, Eleanor and Franklin were living in New York City, so Greenwich Village became Eleanor's refuge. The neighborhood was a hotbed for the Bohemian lifestyle in the 1920s and soon became the go-to hangout for Eleanor and her new adopted family: political, feminist lesbians. She didn't set out with the intention of making friends with a bunch of lesbians specifically, but those were the people who shared Eleanor's political beliefs, and she went with it. And it just so happened that all those queer women helped lead Eleanor down a path of self-discovery.

Two couples—Elizabeth and Esther, and Nan and Marion— each happily accepted Eleanor as a permanent third wheel. She joined these politically active ladies in organizing other women, who had recently won the right to vote.

Eleanor, Nan, and Marion eventually moved in together upstate, not far from the Roosevelt home there, in a little cottage Franklin called the "love nest." The three were essentially life partners. Nan carved their initials, E. N. M., into the cottage's furniture and Eleanor embroidered the same letters into the linens. The women never revealed if Eleanor was romantically or sexually involved with the couple; all anyone knows for sure is that the friendship was more intense than typical.

"Je t'aime et je t'adore"

Eleanor was already in her late forties by the time Franklin's campaign for the presidency began in earnest. She was justifiably afraid that a win for her husband could mean a loss for her: the end of her feminist activism and any semblance of a private life. Even campaigning on Franklin's behalf instead of staying home to crochet had gotten her criticized for stepping out of a woman's place and into the political sphere.

Then Lorena Hickok came into Eleanor's life.

Nicknamed "Hick," Lorena was an up-and-coming Associated Press journalist assigned to cover the would-be first lady during FDR's presidential campaign. Cigar-smoking, work-boots-wearing, poker-playing Lorena had only ever dated women. The two ladies hit it off, bonding over late-night talks, and Lorena's priority quickly became Eleanor as a person instead of journalistic subject. Unbeknownst to the public, she got her own room to sleep in at the White House for whenever she was in town, right next to Eleanor's.

Putting It to Paper

When the two women were apart, they wrote each other letters every single day (which was a lot, before it became normal to send twenty texts a minute), and Eleanor often signed her letters "*Je t'aime et je t'adore.*" Years later, after Eleanor's death, Lorena burned hundreds of the saved notes because, as she told Eleanor's daughter, Anna, "Your mother wasn't always *discreet* in her letters to me." The surviving sixteen thousand pages of correspondence between them were released in 1978, ten years after Hick's death, as she requested.

March 9, 1933 (E.R. to H.)
"My pictures are nearly all up & I have you in my sitting room where I can look at you most of my waking hours! I can't kiss you so I kiss your picture good night & good morning!"

January 22, 1934 (H. to E.R.)
"Dearest, it was a lovely weekend. I shall have it to think about for a long, long time. Each time we have together that way— brings us closer, doesn't it?"

January 27, 1934 (E.R. to H.)
"Gee, what wouldn't I give to talk to you & hear you now, oh, dear one, it is all the little things, tones in your voice, the feel of your hair, gestures, these are the things I think about & long for."

April 19, 1934 (H. to E.R.)
"Oh, damn it, I wish I could be there when you feel as you did Sunday night and take you in my arms and hold you close.

Well, I'll try to make you happy every minute while I'm there in May—"

May 2, 1935 (E.R. to H.)
"I know I've got to stick. I know I'll never make an open break & never tell F.D.R. how I feel."

The letters reveal that Eleanor and Hick dreamed about having their own place one day and that they were ridiculously into each other right from the start. They even once took a road trip without any Secret Service agents in tow, after Eleanor promised she'd take a gun with her for protection (she kept it unloaded at the bottom of the trunk).

Another Changing Partnership

Lorena encouraged Eleanor to make the role of first lady into something it had never been before. At Lorena's suggestions, Eleanor held weekly press conferences exclusively for female reporters (FDR's only allowed men) and started writing a daily syndicated column she used as a policy soapbox—both firsts for a first lady.

As time passed and Franklin continued proving himself a formidable president, the women began to fight. The magic of their romance wore off and Lorena quit her AP job since she could no longer objectively report on her subject. While Lorena's career and finances started to tank, Eleanor was making a name for herself as a political force through the office of the first lady. Eleanor was everything to Lorena, but Lorena was fast becoming just one facet of Eleanor's complex, full life. In the years to come, Eleanor would become a force for global diplomacy, as a delegate to the United Nations and as one of the creators of the first Universal Declaration of Human Rights.

The first lady would send Hick gifts like lingerie or a dried rose from a place they had spent time together to make her feel better, but it rarely worked. What Hick really needed was cash; she had become completely financially dependent on Eleanor, who sent her money, food, and hand-me-down clothes, even after Lorena had moved in with a new female partner.

Eleanor and Lorena continued to write to each other for three decades, and always signed off with phrases like "I love you with all my heart." Though it was Eleanor's husband who famously said the only thing to fear is fear itself, it was the first lady and Hick who demonstrated fearless love. For them, it made all the difference.

BAYARD RUSTIN
1910–1987

tl;dr MLK's right-hand man fights his way out
of the shadows (nonviolently)

The Kentucky heat was oppressive. Bayard loosened his red tie as he boarded the Louisville–Nashville bus. While Bayard fumbled around for his ticket, a white child sitting on its mother's lap in the front seat reached up to play with his tie like it was a dangling toy. The baby's mother slapped its hand away, telling her child not to touch Bayard while referring to him with a racial slur that hit like a second blow.

Bayard, a Northerner, wasn't used to traveling in the South or to encountering the open bigotry that came with it. Shocked and saddened, he headed to the back of the bus to take his seat in the section reserved for black people.

The incident changed something in Bayard that day in 1942. As he sat there, he turned to a black couple next to him and asked, "How many years are we going to let that child be misled by its mother?" The couple ignored him—but Bayard couldn't ignore his inner voice telling him that what he was experiencing was wrong. He decided he would never again let Jim Crow laws dictate where he sat on a bus.

And there was no time like the present to get started.

Bayard stood up, walked forward, and took a seat in the whites-only section. At every stop the driver told him to move, but Bayard said later, "my conscience would not allow me to obey an unjust law." The situation went from bad to worse when the driver called the police.

Four officers boarded the bus thirteen miles north of

Nashville, and when Bayard still refused to get up, the first blows came. They beat him in front of the other passengers, trying to teach him his place.

After the ride in the back of the police car, Bayard was forced to walk between two rows of policemen facing each other on his way into the station. He was tossed from side to side, his clothes ripped, his body bruised. In response, Bayard did something the police had never seen before: nothing.

Bayard was practicing nonviolent disobedience: with each push and hit, he refused to respond with force and instead explained he wouldn't meet violence with violence.

One of the policemen shouted at the calm and defiant resister: "N——, you're supposed to be scared when you come in here!"

But if Bayard was, he certainly didn't show it.

America's Gandhi

Bayard had always been the kind of guy who saw the glass as half full, no matter how many times life knocked the glass over. He believed with all his heart in the big ideas of peace and justice, and he'd spent his whole life trying to fill the world with a bit more of each. As a black man who loved other men, he'd known discrimination all too well during his own life, and he was determined to change that for others.

In 1948, six years after the incident on the bus, Bayard traveled to India to study Gandhian nonviolence. He was convinced it was the way forward for the civil rights movement in the United States. But it was a hard sell, since the National Association for the Advancement of Colored People (NAACP) thought the tactics were weak. Even without the organization's support, Bayard kept practicing his nonviolent protest techniques, though it meant getting arrested regularly for civil disobedience. He didn't need the NAACP or anyone else to agree with him—he was going to do what he thought was right, no matter what.

Of course, it can be difficult to follow your moral compass when the law thinks your sexual identity makes you inherently immoral. . . . Bayard was arrested for hooking up with another man in the back of a car in Pasadena. He pleaded guilty to "sex perversion" and spent two months in jail. When he got out, he was fired from his job at the Fellowship of Reconciliation, an interfaith peace organization. It seemed no one was willing to stand by him despite all he'd done for racial civil rights.

Bayard had known from an early age that he was attracted to men, and he didn't hide it. He was true to himself through and through—from politics to personal relationships. The prison psychiatrist's final evaluation of him at the end of his two-month sentence says it all: "This man impresses me as a confirmed homosexual whose conceit is so extreme and whose homo traits are so deep in the personality, that combining the two features he could not refrain from further homosexual acts."

Bayard had a couple of long-term relationships but claimed he was more into sex than connection and commitment. He didn't have time for things like that—he was already married to the cause.

Free at Last

Bayard eventually resumed his fulfilling work as an organizer and became an adviser to Martin Luther King Jr. Through his passion he convinced Dr. King to make the movement non-violent. Dr. King would have to give up the armed guards protecting his family's home (an understandable precaution, given the threats MLK received). Bayard convinced him to leave the guns out of it. Nonviolence meant nonviolence. Period.

Even with the shadow of the California arrest looming large and dark in his past, Bayard was still chosen as a leader of the most important organizing project of his life: the 1963 March on Washington for Jobs and Freedom. Bringing together such a huge number of people in a time before the Internet was an astonishing feat. Still, when the day arrived—August 28, 1963—no one knew how it would go. Bayard wasn't even sure how many people would really come. That morning, with just the first few hundred people trickling in, the press asked

Bayard where the promised big crowd was. Bayard carefully consulted a piece of paper and told the reporters that everything was going according to plan. . . . Never mind that the paper was blank and he was just bluffing. Secretly, he was terrified that the thousands he hoped for wouldn't turn up.

Bayard needn't have worried.

It wasn't just thousands who showed up; a *quarter million* people arrived to participate in the march. And even with a huge crowd in attendance and racial tensions so high, Bayard's push for a peaceful gathering held strong. He stood right behind Dr. King at the Lincoln Memorial during the now-famous "I Have a Dream" speech and read the demands of the march—including civil rights legislation to end school segregation—to the crowd himself. Less than a year later, the Civil Rights Act of 1964 was signed into law.

Finally, Bayard was given his due. He was featured in *Time* and *Newsweek* and became an internationally respected name. He went on to consult for the US government and worked for peace and social justice globally, from the Middle East to Africa.

At Last, Love

At age sixty-five, Bayard met Walter Naegle, a fellow idealist. The relationship was the first serious romance for both men;

they settled down in New York City and spent the final decade of Bayard's life together. Walter encouraged Bayard to apply his lifetime of civil rights experience to the queer cause.

Walter was thirty-eight years younger than Bayard, and since same-sex marriage wasn't anything more than a distant dream at the time, they had no way to protect their relationship and ensure Walter could inherit Bayard's home when he died. So they did what many other same-sex couples did to create a legal tie between them: Bayard adopted Walter as his son. Sounds weird, but before marriage equality, this was one of the only ways two men could circumvent laws that prevented them from doing married-couple things, like leaving each other a family inheritance. Even this legal roundabout didn't help in the last moments of Bayard's life, when Walter was denied entry to his beloved's room at the hospital.

Bayard wasn't able to see the incredible progress made for queer rights after 1987, but Walter witnessed it for him. Reflecting on his late partner, Walter said: "Being black, being homosexual, being a political radical, that's a combination that's pretty volatile and it comes along like Halley's Comet. Bayard's life was complex, but at the same time I think it makes it a lot more interesting."

ALAN TURING
1912–1954

tl;dr A STEM prodigy invents the modern computer
to save lives during World War II

How had things gotten so mixed up?

Less than three weeks ago, Alan had reported a burglary to the police. *He* had been the victim of a crime in his own home. But after a short investigation, detectives were quick to decide that it was Alan who was the criminal: The last man Alan had let into his house was a guy named Arnold, and Alan admitted it hadn't been a professional or, ummm, totally *platonic* visit. And guys having sex with guys in 1950s England? Illegal. So illegal, in fact, that getting convicted meant up to two years in prison.

Once the cops found out Alan had committed "gross indecency contrary to Section 11," they dropped their burglary investigation and set their sights on a bigger crime: prosecuting Alan for his homosexuality. When they confronted Alan about the nature of his relationship with Arnold, he spilled everything. The police were shocked by his lack of shame: "He was a real convert," said Detective Wills. "He really believed he was doing the right thing."

A Love of Science . . . and More

Alan had lived relatively openly—taking a risk by doing so—as a gay man in Britain up until his arrest in 1952. He wasn't ashamed of who he was. But for all of Alan's brilliant calculations as a mathematician, he had severely underestimated how seriously the police would take his admission of "indecency."

His own sexuality might have seemed like no big deal to Alan because he'd been comfortable with his attractions from a young age. He had fallen hard for a guy named Christopher Morcom in high school. They had a geeky romantic relationship built on stargazing and chemistry experiments and a mutual love of math and science. Seventeen-year-old Alan was crushed when Christopher died suddenly of tuberculosis. As a kind of dedication to his lost first love, Alan devoted himself to STEM studies. Math and science were his only other true loves for the rest of his life.

As time went on, Alan began to wonder if there was a way to make a machine that could house the human mind—almost as a way to get Christopher back, even though his body was gone. Next thing Alan knew, he was publishing groundbreaking papers on artificial intelligence and theoretical computer science; he even went abroad to get his PhD from Princeton. Those who studied and worked with Alan recognized they had a genius in their midst (albeit an awkward, strange genius). Alan's heart was closed once Christopher was gone, but his brain never stopped going.

Machine vs. Machine

In Alan's time, "computer" was a job title for a person who literally computed by solving math problems. He believed there could be a machine that could compute *anything*—not just math but an infinite diversity of tasks. His idea for a "universal machine" would serve as the basis for computers as we know them today, but it was radical in the 1930s. While his papers on the topic were well received, the idea of a universal machine was as theoretical as time travel.

Alan wasn't destined to spend his life theorizing about the future. War was looming, and Alan was recruited by the British government to use his brain for a different goal. He reported to Bletchley Park, the government's HQ for code-breaking work, in 1939—the day before Britain declared war on Germany. He and the other analysts got along, though they thought Alan was odd because he did things like wear a gas mask while riding his bike to protect against the pollen. He always looked like he had just rolled out of bed, and he had the funny habit of running everywhere—even going to places like London from Bletchley (a distance of more than fifty miles). And ultimately, running did become more than a hobby; Alan qualified to run the marathon in the 1952 Olympics.

At Bletchley, Alan wasn't secretive about his sexual orientation and no one seemed to have a big problem with it. He hit on a couple of guys while working there, but neither was interested. Fortunately, everyone was more focused on Alan's ideas than his personal life. The Brits hoped Alan and his team could do the impossible: crack the Enigma code the Nazis used to communicate where and when their U-boats would go. Nazi U-boats were blowing up Allies' naval vessels at an alarming rate. These submarines were nearly undetectable in the water, and their torpedoes were taking down hundreds of Allied ships.

Others at Bletchley Park were skeptical about Alan's "universal machine" idea, but after months of trial and error, the "Bombe," as the computer was called, was eventually able to decode Enigma messages . . . really, really slowly. At first it took weeks to translate a transmission; by the time Alan decoded a message, the ship in question had long been sunk. He persisted, though, and managed to cut the time down from weeks to days until the day in May 1941—one year and eight months after he arrived at Bletchley—when the team began being able to read the Germans' dispatches almost instantly. For the second half of 1941, U-boat attacks weren't half as effective as they'd been during the first part of the year, and Alan's genius saved countless lives.

Alan was crushing the code-breaking game, but 1941 heralded considerably less success in his romantic life. That year, he made his one and only attempt at a serious relationship after Christopher. He proposed to coworker Joan Clarke, who said yes. He then told her about his "homosexual tendencies"; she was accepting and continued the engagement anyway. But Alan eventually broke it off because he felt he couldn't force himself or Joan to go through with a sham marriage.

The Invisible Man

More code-breaking complications came up throughout the remaining years of the war, and Alan worked tirelessly on all of them. But his contributions to the Allied victory in World War II were dismissed as soon as he was convicted of "gross indecency" after the burglary brought his sexuality to light in 1952. Being a criminal meant he lost all his security clearances and couldn't work in code-breaking for the government again.

For his official sentence, Alan was given a choice: prison or chemical castration. To continue his work as best he could, he chose the latter. This punishment involved being forced to take estrogen for a year, with the goal of dulling his libido and therefore "curing" his homosexuality. Though the treatment caused Alan to become impotent and grow breasts, it didn't change the way he felt about men.

With his career in shambles and his life's work stunted, Alan committed suicide by cyanide poisoning in 1954 (though some believe his death was accidental). Since his code-breaking work had been top secret, Alan wasn't publicly recognized for his contribution to the war effort until records from Bletchley were declassified decades later. Queen Elizabeth II officially pardoned him for his "crime" in 2013, but it was too little too late for one of Britain's greatest minds.

JOSEF KOHOUT
1915–1994

tl;dr One of the only gay survivors of the Holocaust ever to share his story

Every day of Josef's life in the concentration camp had been a nightmare—and today looked like it would be even worse. Earlier, Josef had nearly collided with a homophobic camp commander in the common room, and the commander outrageously accused Josef of hitting him. Josef's punishment? Tree hanging, one of the most-dreaded abuses inflicted on prisoners. It involved tying a man's hands behind his back, then stringing him up on a hook attached to a pole. The victim's body weight pulled on his shoulders and put him in excruciating pain. Now, here was Josef: trapped in the barracks with his hands bound behind his back, his mind racing with fear.

Just at the moment Josef was about to be strung up on the hook, one of the camp officers walked over and whispered into the ear of the man carrying out the sentence.

Everything stopped. The rope around Josef's hands was cut and he was let go. He walked away still shaking, grateful that his not-so-secret former lover had used his power to save him.

Grabbed by the Gestapo

Part of a close Catholic family, Josef had led a happy life in Vienna before World War II started. He was nineteen when he came out to his mother. "It's your life and you must live it," she replied. "I've suspected it for a long time anyway. You have no need at all to despair. . . . Whatever happens, you are my son." With such a loving, accepting attitude from his family, Josef was never afraid to be himself.

Even once Hitler was appointed chancellor of Germany in 1933, Josef still didn't think he had anything to fear, so he was confused when the Gestapo showed up at his home one day and told him to come to their headquarters. Had something happened at his college? Students were always getting in trouble with the Gestapo for various protests and resistance demonstrations. But when twenty-two-year-old Josef arrived for his meeting at Gestapo headquarters, the man there asked him flat out: "You are a queer, a homosexual, do you admit it?"

Josef denied it, shocked at the accusation (not because it was untrue, of course, but because he'd been discreet—or so he thought). But the Gestapo had proof: a photo of Josef and his boyfriend, Fred. The picture showed them smiling at the camera with their arms around each other's shoulders, like friends. But it was Josef's writing on the back of the photo from Christmas 1938 that sealed his fate: "In eternal love and deepest affection."

Josef was arrested and quickly convicted of violating Paragraph 175 of the German criminal code, which stated "a male who commits lewd and lascivious acts with another male or permits himself to be so abused for lewd and lascivious acts shall be punished by imprisonment." Josef was branded a "175er," like all those accused of violating Paragraph 175. He wouldn't see home again for six years.

Sachsenhausen

As part of the effort to dehumanize prisoners in the concentration camps, Nazis classified people with tattooed numbers and colored badges corresponding to each person's crime. The crime of being Jewish, for example, meant wearing a yellow star, while the crime of homosexuality was designated by a pink triangle.

Josef was put into a pink-triangle barracks at the Sachsenhausen camp in Oranienburg, Germany, where the rules were different from those in other barracks. Men there were treated like sexual deviants; they had to sleep with the lights on and with their hands over the covers to make sure nothing sexual went on. None of them were allowed to go near other barracks. As an introduction to camp life, they spent six days shoveling snow with their bare hands, moving it from one side of a road to the other. The slogan on the camp gate reminded them: "Work will set you free."

Josef was then assigned to what was known as "the death pit" for his work detail, which involved pushing wheelbarrows of dirt up a steep incline and out of the pit. Since the workers were so starved and weak, every day several would collapse midway up the hill. Their wheelbarrows would roll back and crush them, then career into the others below—giving the death pit its name.

Intent on making it out alive, Josef found a way to get extra food rations to help him survive: a *kapo*—a fellow prisoner given authority over other prisoners—propositioned Josef about exchanging preferential treatment for sexual favors. The prevailing attitude of those in power at the camps was that a man might be in need of an "emergency outlet" because no women were available; it was okay as long as that man wasn't gay outside of this situation. If love had been involved, these acts would have been magically transformed into the filthy sin of homosexuality. Josef was disgusted by the idea of performing sex acts on anyone under these conditions, but he did what he had to do to survive.

After just a few weeks of his arrangement with the *kapo*, Josef was transferred to another camp as part of the routine reshuffling of prisoners. Whatever safety Josef had managed to carve out for himself could be totally obliterated by the move.

Flossenbürg

Josef spent the next five years at Flossenbürg. What he witnessed there is almost unbelievable: Prisoners' bodies hanging as "decorations" from a Christmas tree. Naked men whipped to death while a commander masturbated at the sight of it. Forced trips to a brothel full of imprisoned Jewish and Romany girls—one of the Nazis' attempts to cure homosexuality. At one point the camp received so many shipments of new prisoners marked for extermination that the amount of blood flowing out of the firing squad's drains turned the local pond completely red.

Here, too, Josef managed to find someone to look out for him in exchange for sex. An SS sergeant approached Josef on his first day in the camp, simply asking, "You want to come with me?" Josef said yes right away, knowing exactly what he meant. The sergeant protected Josef from beatings and got him extra food and safer work details. In a world where hard labor could be as deadly as the gas chambers, that last "perk" may have been the biggest.

During his time at Flossenbürg, the handsome Josef had multiple kapos fight over him. A Hungarian Romany kapo even paid off his rivals to have Josef all to himself. Josef later wrote that he came to care for some of these men—almost—because they saved him from torture. His life in the camp was still brutally hard, dangerous, and miserable, but Josef knew others had it far worse.

Getting Out

While at Flossenbürg, Josef accomplished something few 175ers ever did: he became a *kapo* himself. He was put in charge of a work detail making Nazi airplanes for the war. Josef had a couple of dozen prisoners under his command during the day, mostly young men who had the same *arrangement* with someone in power as he did. They all spoke different languages, so Josef needed a way to get everyone to finish the assembly tasks by the end of the day and avoid punishment. His solution? Number the parts rather than name them. It worked! Josef's group always finished their projects with time to spare. And because Josef had earned trust as a *kapo*, he and his men were able to spend their "free" time unsupervised. Rest and recuperation were an almost unheard-of luxury in the camps, and the downtime for Josef and his men saved lives: the men assigned to Josef all survived while under his supervision.

Liberation finally arrived in 1945. Josef went home to Vienna and was reunited with his mother. He learned that his father had killed himself in the middle of the war, leaving a note that read, "God protect our son!"

Josef tried returning to college, but memories of the camp kept creeping up on him during lectures. After those six years it was surreal to go back to normal. Josef wasn't eligible for government compensation like other survivors because homosexuality was still a crime in Austria until 1971, so he got an office job that paid the bills and life went on. He never saw Fred again—and he never found out who gave the photo of the two of them to the Gestapo.

Josef was lucky to be free; thousands of pink-triangle prisoners were transferred to regular German prisons after being released from Nazi concentration camps. Astoundingly, Paragraph 175 wasn't fully repealed in Germany until 1994.

Josef lived out a full life in Vienna beside longtime partner Wilhelm Kroepfl. He forever kept his badge (pink triangle number 1896) in a box in a closet.

JOSÉ SARRIA
1922–2013

tl;dr A "royal" drag queen takes on the
San Francisco government

If you were a drag queen in the 1950s, Halloween was basically a national holiday. In San Francisco, as in many cities around the country, October 31 was the only day that anti-cross-dressing laws weren't in effect. But at twelve midnight on November 1, the San Francisco Police Department was there to round up anyone still in gender nonconforming garb and load them into the waiting paddy wagons.

José, a drag queen famous for his act throughout SF, had had enough. This year was going to be different. In the months leading up to Halloween, he looked up the exact wording of California's cross-dressing prohibition, got an idea, and got to work. Throughout October he gathered the materials he needed to carry out his plan (felt, glue, safety pins, scissors) and then distributed his handiwork around the community.

When Halloween night came, the typical wild party was under way at the Black Cat, the bar where people flocked to see José perform in drag. As usual, the police rolled up at midnight, but instead of scattering, the queens stood their ground.

An officer went up to one queen and told her she'd have to come with him.

"What's the charge, officer?" she asked.

"You're a man in girls' clothes. That's a violation of code."

"But officer, the law clearly states that it is unlawful to dress with intent to deceive. Looky here." She pointed to the cat-shaped felt button attached to her dress. It read, "I am a boy." "There is no intent to deceive, officer," the queen recited, following José's plan. "I am stating my sex clearly for all to see."

Not a single person wearing one of José's badges was arrested that night. For the first time they could remember, the queens had a win in their column.

Great Expectations

Handsome José hadn't set out to become an activist drag queen. Originally, he'd intended to be a teacher.

When the United States entered World War II, José wanted to serve—staying on the sidelines for any reason would have been embarrassing and dishonorable for a patriotic American guy. But there was a problem: to serve in any branch of the military, you had to be at least five feet tall and weigh at least one hundred pounds. José was too small on both counts, just under five feet and shy of ninety pounds. Still, José was determined to serve. He first tried getting into the navy (they had the most attractive uniforms) and then his next choice, the Marines (the second most attractive uniforms). Both rejected the slight Latino. Desperate, José showed up to an army recruiting station and told the man in charge he was willing to do anything to get in. The major asked him out to lunch, and after a few hours in a nearby hotel room, the major signed up José as a five-foot, one-hundred-pound soldier.

When the war ended, José did go to college to pursue his goal of becoming a teacher. But that dream was dashed when he was arrested for solicitation in a hotel bathroom by an undercover cop, a charge he later said was invented to prosecute him for being gay. With that on his record, there was no chance of working in schools. José dropped out and had to find a new career.

The Nightingale of Montgomery Street

Naturally, with military experience and some higher education under his belt, José's career search led him to . . . drag opera performer? José became a female impersonator, a man who identified as male but sometimes performed as a woman. When he started performing at the Black Cat in the 1940s, he introduced "drag opera" to the crowd . . . who went wild when José took the stage, breaking the cross-dressing law every time. She'd squeezed her curves into a long, tight dress and always wore her signature red stilettos. Her tenor voice was beautiful, but her overdramatic acting was what stole the show—especially when she performed *Carmen*. José would flirt with the guys in the crowd and redo the dramatic death scene as many times as the audience wanted.

But José was so much more than the entertainment. Every performance ended with a pep talk in which José would counsel the audience, telling them what they never heard anywhere else: being gay isn't wrong; believe in yourself, and work to change the system. "United we stand," she'd say. "Divided they will catch us one by one." Then she'd lead the group, holding hands, in singing "God Save Us Nelly Queens" to the tune of "God Save the Queen" (also the basis for "My Country 'Tis of Thee"). They'd direct the last verse to the police station across the street, to the local men who had been arrested the night before. One man from the Black Cat remembered, tearing up: "José was the first person to ever tell me that I was okay, that I wasn't a second-class citizen."

Even though the show had to go on, José's main venue was always under attack. The California State Alcoholic Beverage Control Department was determined to shut down all the gay bars. In 1956, they revoked the Black Cat's liquor license on the grounds that "lewd acts" took place there. The bar was able to win on appeal, but the next years were marked by a constant struggle to keep the doors open.

José wanted to do something, but he wasn't the type to riot or break the law like other activists. Just like his "I am a boy" move earlier, he again worked within the system in 1961. He decided the only way the gay community was going to get any power was to have an elected official representing them, so he became the first openly gay person to run for office.

He didn't win, but he had a strong showing. Thousands

voted for him for a seat on the San Francisco Board of Supervisors. "I proved my point," José said. "From that day, at every election, the politicians in San Francisco have talked to us." Sixteen years later, Harvey Milk would win the same seat José had run for.

The Empress

José needed to find a new venue where he could perform and spread his message of empowerment once the Black Cat was shut down for good in 1964. He decided to start a nonprofit to serve the queer community, but the requirement for all certified nonprofits to hold an "election of officers" sounded stuffy and boring. True to his style, José decided this organization would instead have an annual coronation of a new emperor and empress, with dukes and duchesses to make up the Royal Court. José wasn't executive director or president of the board; he was Her Royal Majesty, Empress One of San Francisco, José I, the Widow Norton. He was already a queen—why not upgrade to empress?

From that day on, José was royalty in the queer community. The "Widow Norton" referenced Joshua Norton, a San Francisco man who had declared himself emperor of the United States in 1859. José decided he would play the part of the grieving widow of this eccentric man and organized an annual memorial for him at his grave. That event became an extension of the same community José had built at the Black Cat, a place where queer people could be themselves.

José was now the leader of a large court of dignitaries that came to be called the International Court System. As an official nonprofit organization, the ICS served as a link to the queer community for many people, and over the years its members have raised funds for HIV/AIDS services, LGBTQ community centers, Pride parades, and student scholarships. More than sixty chapters of the Court were established across all of North America during the empress's reign, and they're still going strong today.

In 1970, José decided to attend the first coronation being held outside of California, one for the empress of Portland. A royal entourage (okay, two cars) left San Francisco in the morning and parked at a highway rest stop near the Oregon border for lunch. Two bearded men in Victorian dresses exited first, lifted their veils, and began unpacking a banquet from the trunk of the car while two guards positioned themselves by the cars. The ladies draped a lace tablecloth over a picnic table and set out fine china, crystal glasses, and silver utensils. When the places were set, the empress herself stepped regally out of the lead car and waved to the nearby dumbstruck onlookers, who ogled as the posse lunched on fried chicken.

As they approached their destination, the group pulled

over to call the empress of Portland and inform her that the Dowager Empress, Her Most Royal Majesty, José I would soon be arriving at the gates of the city. The Portland Court immediately sent out a caravan of cars led by a winged Cadillac to escort the convoy from the freeway exit into town.

From that moment to the elaborate state funeral that marked José's death at the ripe old age of ninety, it was nothing but the finest for the empress.

DEL MARTIN & PHYLLIS LYON
1921–2008 & 1924–PRESENT

tl;dr Two women in love found the
American lesbian movement

P hyllis couldn't stop staring. A new employee at Pacific Builder and Engineer in Seattle—a journalist like Phyllis— had just walked in for her first day. She looked sharp in her open-toed pumps and green gabardine suit, but the thing that really caught Phyllis's eye was what the woman carried. No female employee at the office had ever waltzed through the door with one of *those* in hand; after all, it was 1950 and there were *rules*. Unspoken rules, but still . . .

Phyllis had to get to know this stranger, who was bold enough to walk through the doors holding a brown leather briefcase.

For Phyllis, it was practically a revolution.

Believe It or Not (Believe It)

If you had told Del and Phyllis on that day in 1950 that they'd eventually spend the rest of their lives together, they wouldn't have believed you. And they definitely wouldn't have believed they'd get *legally married* fifty-eight years later.

Long before the two women met, they were just two people trying to figure out who they were in a world that didn't quite seem to get them. As a child, Del Martin always took on the role of the husband when playing house with other girls. But the way she played house as an adult was a bit more scandalous. When her marriage to a man ended after four years (spurred by her husband's discovering her lesbian love letters), Del began sharing beds with her neighbors . . . or rather, the married women who lived in the houses on either side of hers. When one woman's husband went off to the Middle East for work, he told Del to "take care of" his wife while he was gone. "So I did," remembered Del with a wink in a 2007 documentary.

Phyllis, on the other hand, wasn't quite so forward. As a girl, she thought it would be nice to get to touch another girl's boobs, but since that was clearly never going to be possible, "why worry about it?" She just put it out of her mind. Eleanor Roosevelt was her absolute idol and heroine, but she wanted to grow up to be a pilot like Eleanor's friend Amelia Earhart. That dream was dashed when she found out her imperfect eyesight was a problem. So she became a journalist instead.

While Del and Phyllis were both originally from Northern California, they happened to end up in Seattle working for the same company: Pacific Builder and Engineer, which published reports about construction. Del later revealed that women who worked at PB&E got "titles of editor and assistant editor in lieu of decent pay." The company was a major boys' club, which was part of the reason Phyllis was so intrigued by Del's briefcase-toting appearance in 1950. Phyllis invited the new girl to a party at her house and was curious why Del spent the whole night in the kitchen with the guys, smoking cigars and learning how to tie a tie. Phyllis had no clue what lesbianism was—she had never even heard the word "lesbian" before. Later on, when Del professed to be one, Phyllis was completely shocked.

After a couple of years of Phyllis being Del's "straight friend," they landed in bed together one night. The two women eventually committed to each other in 1953 and moved into an apartment on Castro Street in San Francisco on Valentine's Day. Their goal was to stay together for an entire year—which was tough, given their extremely bumpy start. They had no idea how to make a long-term relationship work, or how to cohabitate. When Del left her shoes in the middle of the floor, Phyllis threw them out the window instead of asking her to move them.

Thankfully, a friend gave them a kitten, and they joked that they stayed together through some tough times because they couldn't have figured out how to divide the cat. When the year was up, neither woman wanted the "experiment" to end. The first year might have been about proving something to themselves, but the next fifty had "something to do with love."

"Only Women Know the Art of Love"

Finding other lesbians in the 1950s was nearly impossible. The only real option was the bar scene, which left women vulnerable to arrest from police raids. Del and Phyllis felt isolated and were desperate to meet other lady-loving women. In 1955, the one lesbian they knew, Rose Bamberger, called them up and invited them into a secret social club of five others. Phyllis and Del were ecstatic (it was all-caps AMAZING) to increase the number of lesbians they knew by 500 percent. Those eight women formed the first lesbian organization in the United States: the Daughters of Bilitis. They named themselves after the nineteenth-century erotic lesbian poem "The Songs of Bilitis," which professed that "only women know the art of love." If one of their meetings was ever raided, they figured they could use the cover of being a poetry club.

In 1957, lawyer Kenneth Zwerin drew up the DOB's application for incorporation and noted they "could have been a society for raising cats" for all anyone knew. At first the club only hosted parties at members' homes. Secrecy was the highest priority—the women didn't have to give a phone number or last name to join. The group also made up a rule, after three women came to a meeting in men's clothing, that "if slacks are worn they be women's slacks." The idea was to avoid looking like—gasp!—lesbians.

After the first year, Del, Phyllis, and a few other women wanted the DOB to take on political organizing. The Daughters split into two groups, and Del and Phyllis's half focused on education, legislation, and litigation, and held monthly meetings. This revamped DOB organized the first national lesbian conference in 1960 in San Francisco, despite pushback from the FBI, CIA, and San Francisco Police Department. The gathering focused on education, with panels of experts explaining what the current state of lesbian acceptance was in various fields.

The DOB also published the United States's first lesbian magazine, *The Ladder*. The mailing list for the eight-page, hand-stapled newsletter was always carried around by one of the DOB members, since a security breach could endanger subscribers. *The Ladder* was being published at a time when the government was actively hunting down homosexuals and prosecuting them for their "crimes." *The Ladder*'s first issue had an article headlined "Your Name Is Safe!" that detailed the legal precedent the DOB would use to argue their list's privacy, and another article that gave legal advice on what to do if caught in a raid.

Like many *Ladder* writers, Phyllis used a fake name—Ann Ferguson—in her byline. But by the time the fourth issue was published, Phyllis announced she had murdered Ann in cold blood and now only Phyllis Lyon remained. She was determined to practice what she preached: living as out. Most women weren't in a position to take that bold step, though. As one subscriber wrote in about *The Ladder*'s call to "come out of hiding": "What a delicious invitation, but oh, so impractical. I should lose my job, a marvelous heterosexual roommate, and all chance of finding work. . . . I would be blackballed all over the city."

NOW and Then

Unfortunate but true: at that time, gay rights groups ignored women's issues, and women's rights groups ignored lesbian issues. The National Organization for Women had created couples memberships so that husbands could support their feminist wives, but when Del and Phyllis joined as a couple, those couples memberships magically disappeared for any pair—lesbian or straight—who tried to join soon afterward. NOW's leadership was afraid dominant stereotypes about man-hating lesbians would hold back their movement if they allowed lesbians to join, so they unsuccessfully tried to discover and kick out all the lesbians. For the next four years, lesbians lobbied hard, and NOW eventually expanded its policy in 1971 to allow them to be members. Del was elected in 1973 as the first open lesbian on NOW's board of directors.

Del and Phyllis did more and more for the lesbian community over the years after they stepped back from the DOB in 1966. They wrote the book *Lesbian/Woman* in 1972, a first-of-its-kind look at lesbianism with stats from *The Ladder*'s reader survey and other research. One of those statistics revealed that among twenty lesbians in a 1971 discussion group, only two said they had *not* attempted suicide as teens. Del and Phyllis became like aunties to lesbians nationwide and responded to countless letters and phone calls from closeted lesbians around the country who got in touch sometimes to say thanks and other times to be talked off the ledge of a suicide attempt. As Lorraine Hansberry, author of *A Raisin in the Sun*, summarized in her four-page letter to the couple in 1957, "I'm glad as heck that you exist."

In 2008, Del and Phyllis were the first same-sex couple to get married in California when the state ban on gay marriage was struck down. Phyllis remarked, "When [we] first got together, we were not really thinking about getting married, we were thinking about getting together. I think it's a wonderful day."

"Ditto," added Del.

The mayor of San Francisco performed the ceremony in City Hall for the two elderly women, who both wore colorful pantsuits. After the nuptials, the ladies went out for a casual lunch, then home to watch TV.

Del passed away two months later, a newlywed.

SYLVIA RIVERA
1951–2002

tl;dr Early leader of the queer rights movement
gets real about the issues

Queens weren't allowed at the Stonewall Inn. The Mafia-owned establishment was already considered a criminal operation, but allowing "cross-dressing" patrons inside would be a whole separate offense. In New York City, and in many cities around the country, strict laws required people to wear a minimum number of clothing items designed for the sex they were assigned at birth. In NYC, that magic number was three. But Sylvia had connections at the Stonewall, so when she showed up on June 27, 1969 wearing zero men's clothes, she was allowed to waltz right in.

It was a typical Friday night in Greenwich Village as people celebrated the start of the weekend. Watered-down booze was served (despite the State Liquor Authority's absurd policy against serving alcohol to homosexuals), while a mix of "sexual deviants" danced to Rolling Stones songs pouring out of the jukebox.

At 1:20 a.m., the bright overhead lights suddenly flicked on, killing the mood. *Police.* Another raid—the ultimate buzz-kill. An uneasiness settled over the crowd as they waited to find out what was going on. Would they be arrested?

One by one, after presenting their IDs, Sylvia and other club goers were allowed out of the Stonewall. But instead of dispersing like they usually did after an all-too-common police raid, they hung around outside. *What's up with everyone still inside?* they wanted to know. The crowd got anxious about what was happening to the people without IDs. Were they being beaten by the police? That happened plenty during these raids.

Tension grew, and passersby who hadn't been inside the run-down bar stopped and joined the crowd. The anger that had been building from years of police harassment rose to the surface as queer people of all stripes were led out to the paddy wagon under arrest—as they often were after a routine raid. Then a butch lesbian was dragged out, struggling against the police who held her. Everything shifted when she yelled to the crowd, "Why don't you guys do something!"

Sylvia was the kind of person to do something. She was tired of the beatings, the discrimination. As the crowd grew restless and started to throw coins at the police, Sylvia was among the first to throw a bottle.

Almost immediately, the police barricaded themselves inside the bar. Molotov cocktails sailed in through the window, and the police started to run out of water and fire extinguishers. A parking meter was used as a battering ram against the door. A thought passed through Sylvia's head: "My God, the revolution is here. The revolution is finally here!"

The Village

Sylvia, who was assigned male at birth, never got a break in life, but she never let it break her. Things were rough right from the start and worsened quickly after her mother committed suicide when Sylvia was just three years old. Ms. Rivera mixed rat poison into a glass of milk, drank it, and gave some to Sylvia. Sylvia didn't like the taste of the milk, so she didn't have much, but afterward she still needed her stomach pumped. One of the last things her mom said, as she lay dying in the hospital, was that she'd wanted to kill Sylvia because she knew her child was going to have a hard life.

That turned out to be a self-fulfilling prophecy, since Ms. Rivera's death left Sylvia's care in the hands of her Venezuelan grandmother. And care for Sylvia she did, if you consider "care" beating her and telling her she was unwanted, in part because she had her father's dark Puerto Rican skin. Dear *viejita* also hated Sylvia's effeminacy—but that didn't stop Sylvia from experimenting with makeup as early as fourth grade. She'd put on makeup after leaving the house in the morning and remove it before coming home to avoid her grandmother's wrath. Resilient, and determined to start living as the girl she was no matter what, Sylvia left home forever when she was just ten years old.

That's when she found Greenwich Village, her true home. It was a hub of possibility for runaway misfits like Sylvia, who fit right in with the other street kids turning tricks to get by. A few drag queens took her under their wing.

Life was dangerous, not just because of the sex work but

because of the police. Cross-dressing and homosexuality were illegal in 1960s New York; you could get picked up for those crimes anytime. Sylvia did all she could to stay out of lockup, which she knew could be more violent for a trans woman than the street was. One time she got into a car with a john who turned out to be an undercover cop; he threatened her with jail unless she took care of him. He had a gun pointed at her and said he'd shoot if she got out of the car. But Sylvia did get out and grandly sashayed away before breaking into a sprint. Another time, an undercover cop was taking her in and she jumped out of the moving car going full speed. And the one occasion she did eventually get arrested and put in a cell, she gave the guy who tried to have his way with her a bite to remember. The other prisoners steered clear of her after that.

Stonewall to Star House

The Stonewall Riots were the spark that ignited the modern LGBTQ rights movement. Sylvia said it was the moment she "saw the world change for me and my people." Just nineteen at the time, Sylvia helped organize new queer rights advocacy groups in the aftermath. But for all her efforts, Sylvia was pissed about the direction those early groups took—like working on a gay rights bill but not including trans rights. After working her butt off for them, Sylvia kept being told to wait her turn. *We'll just get the rights for gay men first, then we'll come for trans women, mmmkay?* It didn't take Sylvia long to figure out they were never coming for her, and it stung. Her own community, not the police or other outsiders, had turned their backs on her during this pivotal time. As Sylvia would often say, "Hell hath no fury like a drag queen scorned."

Sylvia and her best friend, Marsha P. Johnson, started seeing to the trans community's concerns themselves by founding the Street Transvestite Action Revolutionaries. STAR addressed the immediate needs of street kids just barely younger than Sylvia and Marsha. This wasn't organizing petitions; it was finding hungry kids their next meal. Sylvia's and Marsha's income from sex work funded the STAR house, where trans kids could sleep safely off the street and hopefully avoid turning tricks to survive. The STAR kids stole food as their contribution to the house. If only there had been a queer advocacy group that could help. . . . Oh wait, that's right—there was. Sylvia had already worked for them. But when she needed help, they were nowhere to be found.

The Struggle

Annual parades popped up to commemorate Stonewall's anniversary starting in 1970, the year after the infamous raid. It was at one of these events that eventually came to be known as Pride—New York City's 1973 celebration—that Sylvia's struggle was brought into sharp focus. After initially being invited to speak to the crowd, Sylvia was abruptly removed from the program; a lesbian event organizer thought Sylvia's very identity was somehow offensive to cisgender women. Not one to take adversity lightly, Sylvia made her way to the stage anyway as the crowd booed her: "I had to fight my way up on that stage and literally, people that I called my comrades in the movement, literally beat the shit out of me. That's where it all began, to really silence us. They beat me, I kicked their asses." She called out the crowd for their shortcomings, and told them her trans sisters didn't write to the women's movement or the gay movement from jail for help—they wrote to STAR.

"You all tell me, go and hide my tail between my legs. I will no longer put up with this shit. I have been beaten. I have had my nose broken. I have been thrown in jail, I have lost my job, I have lost my apartment for gay liberation, and you all treat me this way? What the fuck's wrong with you all?"

Indeed, Sylvia.

A Movement within a Movement

Sylvia spent the rest of her life working for queer rights, swimming against the current of the mainstream gay rights movement. Ironic as it may seem, her biggest battles came from *inside* the queer community rather than outside it. She fought to give voice to underrepresented groups like trans youth, the incarcerated, and the homeless. She caught everyone who had fallen through the cracks.

Sylvia's struggles with drugs and alcohol led to her own homelessness in her later years, but she never stopped fighting for the movement. Eventually she found a place to live: Transie House, a shelter for transgender people. She found love there, too; Sylvia and Julia Murray became friends first, then lovers and partners in 1999. Sylvia reflected, "I feel that both of us being transgendered, we understand what the other has gone through. We have always been with men, but the men that we have met in our lives haven't been able to give us the sensitivity that we share between ourselves." Being with Julia helped Sylvia stay sober in her final years.

Sylvia was tenacious to the end, even meeting with other activists about passing queer rights legislation while she was dying of liver failure in a hospital bed at the age of fifty. She had said she wanted to live to be a hundred years old so she could spend the time working on the post-1969 revolution and maybe live to see the changes she worked for come true. The trans community is still fighting for what Sylvia worked for, and now they often do so under organizations named for her. Today, anyone who visits the Stonewall Inn (which became the United States's first national monument dedicated to queer history in 2016) will enter from the renamed "Sylvia Rivera Way."

RENÉE RICHARDS
1934–PRESENT

tl;dr A transsexual trailblazer wins a landmark

legal victory

Six-year-old Dick Raskind stood in his bedroom doorway, still as stone. He was listening for any movement in the house, making sure no one was around to catch him. With the coast clear, he scurried down the hallway to his sister's room. Hands shaking, he took a skirt, blouse, shoes, stockings, garter belt, panties, and hat from her drawers and dashed to the bathroom.

Heart racing, Dick changed into the girls' clothes.

That first moment when he saw his reflection in the mirror, he noticed that the clothes were too big and that he didn't look as pretty as he would have liked. But Dick noticed something else, too: he felt so much calmer in these clothes than in his own. So much . . . *better*. As he quickly changed and put the clothes back, the serenity that had come over him disappeared, replaced with guilt. The six-year-old felt he'd been very wrong to do what he'd done . . . but he was also already looking forward to the next time he could do it again.

The "Correct" Life Path

Another quick terminology note: Renée would later look back on her time as Dick as time spent as a man, so we've used male pronouns for Dick before transitioning to Renée, just as Renée does in her self description. Note that, unless otherwise preferred, using the originally assigned pronouns to describe a trans person pretransition is incorrect and disrespectful.

Even though Richard Raskind, as Renée was known for the first half of her life, clearly knew who he really was from an early age, finding the courage to let out Renée would take years. The road would be long and very difficult, but it was the path Dick had to walk to be true to himself.

As a teenager, Dick found a copy of Lili Elbe's biography, *Man into Woman*. Once he realized a physical transition was possible, he knew it was what he wanted. To Dick, genital surgery was the only thing that would make him a woman. But it wasn't as easy as just booking an OR for the next available date (it still isn't). So Dick would live with his secret long before he was actually able to consider surgery. Keeping Renée hidden would be a source of depression, anxiety, and turmoil through Dick's twenties and thirties.

During childhood and adolescence, no one knew about Renée. In college, Dick's girlfriend found his dresses and made him promise he wouldn't do any of that "stuff" while she was away for vacation off campus. But the divide in his double life only grew wider from there. Dick began going out as Renée—not where anyone he knew would see him, but still in public. With an eye toward a future when he could and would have sex transition surgery, he began taking estrogen shots under a doctor's supervision and dressing as Renée more regularly. Despite beginning to embrace his secret life, Dick maintained the same facade he had since high school: a macho, motorcycle-riding ladies' man who loved to play tennis.

Following college, med school, and a federally required stint in the navy (he had deferred his draft so he could serve as a doctor after his residency), Dick chose one of the very limited options for physical transitions in the 1960s: going to Casablanca, Morocco, for surgery. No doctors in the United States were even offering transition surgery at the time. But when Dick got to Casablanca and it was actually time to go into the clinic, he couldn't bring himself to do it. He was afraid of the physical risks and what life afterward would be like. Cash in hand, he flew back to New York.

When he returned home from Morocco, Dick's doctors in New York got cold feet and refused to continue his estrogen injections. They weren't opposed to people undergoing transition surgery, but they felt it was an ethical violation to allow a successful man—a doctor, no less—to "throw away" a seemingly good life for a sex change. Good thing Dick was looking for a moral judgment from these guys. . . .

Around the same time, a friend introduced Dick to a woman named Barbara. Feeling defeated, he gave up on transitioning and committed himself to a traditional life. After dating her for six months, Dick married Barbara (who thought of her new husband as a typical red-blooded American man and never suspected the secret identity he'd harbored for so long) and grew into his role as wealthy, hetero eye-surgeon guy, and two years later, he was a new father. Renée was locked away, and Dick even got breast reduction surgery to undo the effects of the estrogen. It was what his doctors wanted . . . and it made Dick absolutely miserable.

Transitions

This perfect-on-the-outside life couldn't last. Unable to live as Renée, Dick was on the verge of killing himself. He divorced Barbara, quit his job, and finally went through with the reassignment surgery in 1975—thirty-two years after he'd first donned women's clothing. Lying on the table about to go under, he reflected on the name he had chosen at a young age. Back then, he didn't know that Renée translated to "reborn" in French. The name—and the surgery—seemed like fate.

When Renée finally began to live as herself, she was already in her forties. Barbara was "disgusted." Renée's sister thought it was a huge mistake. Her friends had urged her not to do something "so drastic"—though it was a little late to turn back. Without support in New York, Renée headed west, where no one would know her past, to start over with a blank slate.

Renée bought a Shelby Cobra, a small but powerful race car, and headed to California. She identified with the car, which was built to go fast but had a very fragile exterior. Once she arrived on the new coast, Renée led a very similar life to Dick's in New York: practicing medicine and playing amateur tennis. She "wanted nothing more than to melt into American society and live happily ever after." That's not *exactly* how things went down.

Renée played in tennis tournaments that were high profile enough to get press coverage, and one reporter went digging about this mysterious newcomer's past. He found the New York medical license for Richard Raskind that had been converted to a California one . . . in Renée's name. When the story broke in 1977, Renée was headline news. Female players dropped out of the tournaments Renée was in, refusing to play against a transsexual woman in a women's competition.

To add insult to injury, the US Tennis Association declared that Renée was not allowed to play women's tennis in professional matches until she passed a "sex test" first. If the test determined she had XX chromosomes instead of XY, she could play. Renée refused, arguing: "I'll take a sex test but I'll take a reasonable sex test like a gynecological examination." She was angry that they wouldn't let her play even though she had a document from the New York City Health

Department stating that she was female. The next step Renée took changed the landscape for trans rights: she sued the USTA for her right to play as a woman without taking their chromosome test—and won.

Game, Set, Match

Two months after winning the court case that guaranteed her the legal right to play as a woman, Renée was the first out trans person to play in the US Open. She was forty-three years old, and her pro tennis career was just beginning. She toured the world for four years, having fun with the other female tennis players on the circuit. She says it was like the adolescence Renée never got to have.

After she retired, Renée coached the newly out-as-bisexual Martina Navratilova (who later came out as a lesbian) for a while and then eventually moved back to New York. She began working as a doctor again at the very same place that had employed Richard Raskind years earlier. She had come full circle.

Today Renée makes her home in a cottage in upstate New York, commuting in for her ophthalmologist job. She finally lives the quiet, mostly anonymous life she always wanted. Renée attends the US Open every year as just another fan of the game.

HARVEY MILK
1930–1978

tl;dr The beloved leader of a gay political revolution

"You get the first bullet the minute you stand at the microphone" was the message on the postcard that had come in the mail last week. Harvey regularly received death threats like this one, and he always laughed them off outwardly no matter how he felt inside. But would today be the day Harvey's enemies finally made good on their promises to kill him? Would the 1978 Gay Freedom Day Parade in San Francisco mark the end of his crusade for gay rights—and his life?

When Harvey stepped up to the microphone at the Freedom Day celebration, he spoke to the assembled crowd about the battle against Proposition Six, the proposed law that would ban homosexuals from teaching in California schools. Freedom. Equality. These were the pursuits that made jeopardizing his life worthwhile.

> Let me remind you what America is.
>
> Listen carefully:
>
> On the statue of Liberty, it says, "Give me your tired, your poor, your huddled masses yearning to be [sic] free. . . ."
>
> In the Declaration of Independence, it is written: "All men are created equal and they are endowed with certain inalienable rights. . . ."
>
> And in our national anthem, it says: "Oh, say does that star-spangled banner yet wave o'er the land of the free."

For . . . all the bigots out there: That's what America is. No matter how hard you try, you cannot erase those words.

Hundreds of thousands of queer people and their allies erupted into applause. Harvey stepped down from the podium, glowing from the crowd's energy and relieved to have survived another public appearance. Let the haters mail all the death threats they wanted; California's first openly gay elected official wasn't going anywhere.

The Mayor of Castro Street

Harvey started off just a big-eared Jewish kid from Long Island who grew up and decided to go work for corporate America. But when the liberal hippie wave of the sixties and seventies hit, Harvey got swept up in it. He grew his hair long and moved from New York City to San Francisco to start a completely new life with his lover of three years, Scott Smith. Though twenty years younger than Harvey, Scott had been living the life of a free spirit for much longer. After bumming around his Mississippi hometown and taking too much LSD, long-blond-haired Scott got bored and moved to Greenwich Village at twenty-two years old and met Harvey.

With New York behind them, Harvey and Scott drove around California in Harvey's Dodge Charger, passing the days lazily, living off savings, and spending most nights in sleeping bags under the redwoods with their adopted dog, the Kid. They spent their last $1,000 (equivalent to more than $5,000 today) to settle down and start a camera shop on Castro Street in San Francisco—soon to become the queer capital of the United States—even though neither of them was trained in anything related to photography. It didn't really matter what the store sold; Harvey just loved the idea of having their own business underneath the apartment they rented. He even put a sign in the storefront window: "Yes, We Are Very Open."

The Castro district of San Francisco was changing fast. Every week dozens of gay people from around the country were making the pilgrimage to the Promised Land and staying. Traditional shops owned by conservative folks went under as new gay establishments sprang up in their place. But not everybody was happy about the shift, and violence against homosexuals became as common in 1970s California as faded bell-bottoms and tie-dyed shirts. The police weren't much help, either. The very people who should have been protecting innocent victims of hate crimes instead patrolled the Castro to raid gay bars. (The motto to "protect and serve" apparently excluded queer people.) Unwilling to be victimized, gay men got organized to protect themselves and started carrying whistles so they could call out for help if they got in trouble. One night, Harvey and a friend were in the Castro when they heard a whistle blowing. They both ran to the victim of the latest beating and then Harvey chased down the attacker. When he caught the bigot, Harvey didn't respond with violence; instead, he let him go with a warning: "Tell all your friends we're down here waiting for them."

After years of being closeted on the East Coast, Harvey became more and more active within the gay community. He believed the way to make change was from the inside, so in 1973 he decided to run for one of the spots on the San Francisco Board of Supervisors, which did the lawmaking for the city. He lost. But two years later, with his hair cut short and his jeans traded in for a suit, he ran again . . . and lost, again. Still! All that campaigning had lit a fire inside Harvey. People were responding to his platform of equality for all (not just gays but all the marginalized groups of San Francisco). He was already making a difference just with his candidacy, and he didn't want to stop.

The same couldn't be said for Scott, who was tired from three solid years of crusading. For both men, life had become about squeezing any small profit they could out of the camera store to put toward the next campaign's signs. The carefree hippie Scott had met in Greenwich Village was gone, and a political machine now lay next to him in bed. Scott had already started sleeping in a separate bedroom, and when the 1975 election was over, he moved out. Harvey had lost a partner—and his campaign manager.

The following year, California voting districts were rezoned and the Castro would be electing its own supervisor to the board. Harvey knew he'd finally win, but it was still a hard fight. Somehow, Harvey found time amid all the campaigning to pick up a cute boyfriend, Jack Lira. Jack moved in with Harvey soon after they met; they exchanged hundreds of love notes over the course of their relationship. Scott was jealous, but Harvey was smitten. When people asked Harvey what he was doing with Jack (who they considered a hot mess), he'd just wink and say the sex was great.

Elected

When Harvey won the election by a good margin, the celebration in San Francisco was epic: Harvey rode down Castro Street on the back of a motorcycle, waving to his fans. He became one of the first openly gay people elected to public office in the country. On day one at City Hall, Harvey walked up the steps with Jack on his arm and said: "You can stand around and throw bricks at Silly Hall or you can take it over. Well, here we are."

And take over he did. Harvey accomplished a ton in his first months in office. As he had promised, he was a supervisor fighting for all communities, not just gays. He especially championed senior citizens, even though he said he would never get to be one himself (see: death threats). He brought up bills that everyone could support, like enacting fines for leaving your dog's poop on the sidewalk. And in the queer community, he was an inspirational figure at a local and national level. He encouraged all queer people to come out even though it was hard, and to have hope above all else. He secured the passage of San Francisco's gay rights ordinance, which would protect gay people from being fired from their jobs or kicked out of their homes just for being gay. Of the whole board, only one supervisor voted against it.

And that supervisor was Dan White. Dan was part of a conservative group of San Franciscans being crowded out of the area by the wave of gay transplants taking over the city. As he put it: "Change is counterproductive when you force it on people. I fear that's where the problem is going to start." Dan knew something about that fear; it had taken root right in his own mind.

November 27, 1978

Eight months after the ordinance was passed, Dan entered San Francisco City Hall through a window, carrying a loaded .38–caliber revolver and extra bullets in his pocket. He walked straight into the mayor's office; Mayor George Moscone was Harvey's political friend who had happily supported the gay rights

QUEER, THERE, AND EVERYWHERE

ordinance. Dan shot the mayor four times, killing him, then left the room as George's still-lit cigarette burned his silk tie.

Dan made his way through the building to the supervisors' offices and stopped at Harvey's door.

"Harvey, can I see you for a minute?"

"Sure."

Inside Harvey's office, Dan again took out the gun. He shot. Again. And again. The fourth bullet entered the base of Harvey's skull. Then, to be sure his mission was complete, Dan moved closer and fired a final shot into Harvey's brain. Harvey was just forty-eight years old.

Dan walked out of the office, nodding a casual hello to another city worker, who had no idea what had just happened, and left.

That night, Scott joined the tens of thousands of San Franciscans who marched silently, each with a lit candle, from the Castro to City Hall. For the San Francisco queer crowd, which often responded to infuriating events by rioting, it was a beautiful, peaceful response to violence.

Legacy

Dan White would serve only five years in prison for the double murder after his defense team successfully argued that depression caused in part by eating junk food had left him mentally incompetent and incapable of premeditation (the infamous "Twinkie defense"). The night after the verdict was announced, the city rioted, shattering the glass doors of City Hall and burning more than a dozen police cars.

The assassination only increased Harvey's impact on the world. He had lived in San Francisco for just eight years and had been a city supervisor for less than one, but his legacy endures decades later. Harvey did everything in San Francisco with an eye on the national gay rights movement and he knew his role as a highly public, very out politician would carry risks. But even with the sure knowledge that he lived with a target on his back, Harvey kept his focus on the movement. "If a bullet should enter my brain," he said in a recording he made just days before his murder, "let that bullet destroy every closet door."

GLENN BURKE
1952–1995

tl;dr Decades before Michael Sam and Jason
Collins, Glenn Burke scores points for queer men
in sports

It was spring training in 1980, and Glenn was excited for Billy Martin to start as the new manager of his team, the Oakland A's. The feeling wasn't remotely mutual—in Billy's eyes, Glenn was batting for the wrong team.

Spring training brought with it all the usual growing pains as players batted, pitched, and fielded away the relative laziness of the off-season. But while the A's were getting back on their game, Glenn was thrown off his. One day in the locker room he overheard Billy say:

"No faggot's going to ever play in my ball club."

A Love of the Game

Raised in Oakland, Glenn was a devout Christian who couldn't get enough of sports. He could have easily gone for a career in basketball instead of baseball (and he later said his only regret was that he should have done just that). Sex wasn't at all a part of Glenn's early life, and he got all his energy out through athletics.

Three years before joining the A's, when Glenn was twenty-three, he had a revelation. He realized there must be a reason why he didn't feel about girls the way other guys seemed to. The only similar feeling he could think of was the crush he'd had on Mr. Mendler, his middle school's glee-club and drama teacher. When the reality of his sexual orientation hit home,

Glenn drove to his old school, found Mr. Mendler, and confessed his feelings. That led to Glenn's first sexual experience; he cried for hours afterward, consumed by the relief of finally understanding himself for the first time. Over the years, Glenn and Mr. Mendler ended up becoming casual friends with benefits.

Glenn was already in the minor leagues when he had his encounter with Mr. Mendler and immediately knew he would have to stay closeted or risk committing "baseball suicide." He moved out of his apartment and into the YMCA so his roommates wouldn't discover his secret if he brought home a guy. Despite all the precautions he took, Glenn knew he would have to be an above-and-beyond ball player as a kind of insurance. If he was the best player on the roster, maybe he'd still have a career even should his secret be discovered.

The Big Leagues

Glenn was called up to the Major Leagues a year later, in 1976. His first team was the Dodgers, famous for racially integrating the team with the first black pro baseball player, Jackie Robinson, twenty-nine years earlier. Glenn, also a black man, couldn't know he was about to test the team's tolerance for diversity once again.

Glenn's future was bright and several baseball insiders

commented on his limitless potential. He performed well for the Dodgers and got along with his teammates, but there was a problem. Tommy Lasorda, one of the team's managers, didn't like the relationship between his son and Glenn. Spunky Lasorda was openly gay, though his father denied it. Glenn and Spunky were superclose despite appearing to be opposites: Glenn was a six-foot macho muscleman nicknamed King Kong, and Spunky was a rail-thin bleached blond obsessed with his tan. They spent their time going out in the Castro in San Francisco and commiserating about Tommy's homophobia. Both men had a great sense of humor; one time, they planned to show up at Tommy's for dinner wearing pigtails. They canceled their prank at the last minute because Glenn was sure "Tommy first would have shot us both in the head. Then he would have had a heart attack and died."

Whether Glenn and Spunky were ever more than barhopping buddies, Glenn never revealed. But their relationship ended abruptly when the Dodgers paid Spunky to never see Glenn again. Glenn was pissed off that Spunky accepted the buyout, and the two never reconciled.

Despite the drama off the field, Glenn was a solid player for the team, with average batting and fielding stats. So when he was called into a meeting with Al Campanis, the team's general manager, Glenn assumed it was to discuss his contract for 1978 and beyond. He was excited to be offered a great deal, but his enthusiasm couldn't have been more misplaced.

Al laid it out plain and simple: marry a woman, or your career with the Dodgers will be in danger. He even offered Glenn $75,000 to get hitched, and told him: "Everybody on this team is married but you, Glenn. When players get married on the Dodgers, we help them out financially." *cough not true cough*

Glenn declined the bribe. The next season he was traded to the lower-ranked A's in exchange for an aging player.

A Secret Revealed

Glenn had lasted four seasons total in Major League Baseball before being blackballed and forced into early retirement at age twenty-seven. Soon after being unceremoniously outed to the A's courtesy of manager Billy Martin, Glenn was released from his contract early.

Though Glenn's sexual orientation wasn't a secret to those inside baseball by 1978, it wasn't until three years after his retirement that the public learned Glenn was gay. But just like his outing to the A's, the confession wasn't on Glenn's terms. And this time, the betrayal was far worse.

The most serious romantic relationship in Glenn's life was with Michael Smith, a controlling man who ultimately took advantage of him. Michael wrote an article for *Inside Sports* magazine called "The Double Life of a Gay Dodger" that went to print in 1982 without Glenn's permission. After its publication, Bryant Gumbel interviewed Glenn on the *Today* show, marking the first time an out gay sports player was seen on TV sets across the United States. At the end of the interview, Glenn gave Gumbel a hat from Glenn's gay softball team, astonishing Gumbel and his viewers.

The High Five

With all the focus on Glenn's sexual orientation, it's easy to forget the man's legacy extends well beyond a short baseball career and coming out. On October 2, 1977, Glenn Burke *co-invented the high five.*

It was a home game for the Dodgers, the last of the regular season. Glenn's teammate Dusty Baker had just hit in a home run in front of forty-six thousand cheering fans. Glenn was next up to the plate and put his hand up to greet Dusty coming into home plate. Dusty recalled: "His hand was up in the air, and he was arching way back, so I reached up and hit his hand. It seemed like the thing to do."

Glenn then hit his first home run in the majors, and Dusty high-fived him on his return. The practice took off in the following years, first within baseball and then in all sports. By 1980, the Dodgers were selling trademarked "High Five"

T-shirts. Glenn's ex, Michael, asserted that it was a gay pride symbol, "a legacy of two men's hands touching."

A Downward Spiral

Unfortunately, there was no happy ending to Glenn's story. He became addicted to cocaine, and his only breaks from living on the streets were spent in jail. He was diagnosed with AIDS in 1993, after which one of his sisters took him in and cared for him until he died of the disease.

On his deathbed, Glenn dictated his memoir to a ghost-writer:

> As I reach my final days, I'd like to be remembered as just a down-to-earth good person. A man that tried to never have a bad thought in his mind. A man who really tried to get along with everybody at all times, no matter what the situation. A man who will always love his friends and family. Despite what people are going to say or write about me after I die, I want it to be known that I have no regrets about how I lived my life. I did the best I could.

MYCHAL JUDGE
1933–2001

tl;dr "The Saint of 9/11" defines American heroism

as a queer, celibate Franciscan friar

The morning of September 11, 2001, dawned sunny and beautiful. Mychal Judge, better known as Father Mike, was in his room in the friary at West Thirty-First Street in Manhattan when a fellow priest who had just watched an airplane crash into the north tower of the World Trade Center burst in to tell him the news.

Father Mike had been serving as chaplain to New York City firefighters for almost a decade when he arrived at the chaotic, tragic scene that morning. Mayor Rudolph Giuliani was one of the first to speak to him: "Mychal, please pray for us." "I always do," Father Mike replied as he ran into the lobby of the north tower with the firefighters. His white FDNY-issued helmet bobbed along in the crowd; Father Mike was no stranger to fires.

But while Father Mike was normally a reassuring presence at the site of a fire, that day he was pale and withdrawn, not making eye contact with anyone. He just paced back and forth, praying. The smell of smoke filled his nose. Every few seconds he could hear a sickeningly loud boom—another person who had jumped from the burning floors above and landed on the entrance canopy, covering the lobby windows in blood. First responders wondered if they might be safer inside the north tower than outside it; at least one firefighter had already been killed by a jumper landing on him.

The mayor and others were evacuating the area. "You

should go, Padre," a firefighter told Father Mike. "I'm not finished" came the reply. Father Mike climbed the stopped escalator to the top of the mezzanine, where he'd been told he was needed to provide comfort. Out the windows he could see the plaza completely covered in clumps that had once been people. Some scraps of clothing, some body parts, and maybe a shoe were all that could still be identified.

Father Mike closed his eyes and called out, "Jesus, please end this right now!" The plate-glass window next to him was sprayed with blood from yet another falling body hitting the pavement as he pleaded again, "Jesus, please end this right now!"

They were the last words Father Mike would ever say.

Following in the Steps of Saint Francis

Father Mike's death certificate was number DM00001-01, the first official casualty of 9/11. No one witnessed his death in the moment after he called out for Jesus at 9:59 a.m., and his body didn't show any physical trauma from falling debris. It's possible that, witnessing such unstoppable horror, he was scared to death.

Father Mike had always wanted to grow up to be a priest, or as he said it as a child, a "peest." He was raised in Brooklyn, the son of Irish immigrants, with the name Robert Emmett

Judge. He'd later choose the priest name Michael and then change the spelling to Mychal to differentiate himself from all the other Father Michaels.

Becoming a Franciscan friar wasn't easy. It took years and years of study, dedication, and isolation before they'd let you in, but Father Mike made it to ordination. Throughout this process—and really, throughout most of his life—Father Mike knew he was attracted to other men. But choosing a celibate life meant he would never act on his feelings, which he thought was best—Father Mike believed personal attachments would keep him from fulfilling his calling to help those in need. He developed passionate crushes on his classmates, but as far as he knew, he was the only one with those feelings. Father Mike didn't see denying his desires as a sacrifice but as a way to be more available to do God's work; unlike some who pledged to serve others but eventually made spouses or children a priority instead, Father Mike was devoted to "welcoming the stranger" as Christians are called to do.

Life as a friar meant taking a vow of poverty, and Father Mike embraced it. If you gifted him a sweater, you'd see it the next day on a homeless man. But even as a man of the cloth, his life was far from quiet. Ministering to New Jersey and New York meant his days were filled more with the sounds of sirens than church bells; he followed first responders to wherever he might be needed in and around the city.

One time he showed up on the scene of a man threatening his wife and children at gunpoint on the second floor of a building. Father Mike hung on to a ladder outside the window with one hand while holding his brown Franciscan robes with the other, trying not to slip. Onlookers were sure someone was going to end up dead, either by fall or by gunshot. The calm friar kept telling the man that they could find another way to work this out, that he didn't really want to do this, that he was a good man. Why didn't he just come downstairs for some coffee? It worked. The man lowered his gun and no one was hurt.

Omnisexual

Father Mike once told a friend that maybe he was omnisexual, drawn to all of God's adult human creations. Gay people who spent time with him thought he was gay, and straight people who spent time with him thought he was straight. Throughout the 1990s, he had a close relationship with Al Alvarado, a nurse from the Philippines. Father Mike was clear with Al from the beginning that he was a groom of Christ, so their relationship would never progress physically. Even emotionally, Father Mike made sure to keep a certain distance from Al so his focus was always on those he served. Al couldn't bring himself to walk away from the relationship, even though he knew he would never be the number one love of Father Mike's life. He once commented that "my rival was God."

The relationship between queer people and the Catholic church was . . . um, *strained* during Father Mike's life, to say the least. The church's view was that homosexuals were sinners and that was the end of it. In the aftermath of the Stonewall Riot in the 1970s, Father Mike joined the effort to create Dignity, a national group of queer Catholics focused on prayer and advocacy. He ministered to queer people at a time when many priests wouldn't. But his calling was also to the general public, and he especially served the homeless faithfully.

In 1986, the Vatican issued a statement calling homosexuality "an intrinsic moral evil" (yikes!) and the strain got worse. Dignity groups were no longer allowed to meet in churches. Father Mike once comforted a fellow gay priest who had tried to stand up for gay rights in the church and was being ostracized, reminding him, "They did the same to Jesus."

"Gay-Related Immune Deficiency"

In the 1980s, Father Mike was led into service of another marginalized group. When the HIV/AIDS epidemic struck the United States, the lack of information led to hysteria. Nurses wouldn't bring HIV/AIDS patients meals into their hospital rooms for fear of catching it. And almost anywhere that would have performed services for the deceased refused to prepare the bodies of or officiate at funerals for those who had succumbed to the disease. Father Mike started the Saint Francis AIDS ministry on Thirty-First Street and mobilized those willing to help. He physically touched HIV/AIDS patients and talked with them when few others would. Once word got around that he was not only willing but very skilled at leading memorial services for those who had died of HIV/AIDS, he traveled across state lines more than once to answer every request.

Becoming the fire chaplain for the FDNY was an adjustment. Working with macho guys who he assumed were homophobes was pretty different from cradling dying queer men in his arms. He quickly became beloved in his new environment, showing up at the scenes of fires and in hospital rooms at any hour when spiritual counsel was needed. He stood with the firefighters and marched with them in Saint Patrick's Day parades, even though the Irish Lesbian and Gay Organization was banned from participating and protested the event.

Waiting on the Other Side

Father Michael Duffy gave the homily at Father Mike's service. The church was packed with guests, including Bill, Hillary, and Chelsea Clinton. Hillary recalled that Father Mike "lit up the White House" when he had led a prayer breakfast there. Father Duffy had a theory about why Mychal had been among the first to perish that day:

> There were between two and three hundred firemen buried there, the commissioner told us that night. Mychal Judge could not have ministered to them all. It was physically impossible in this life but not in the next. And I think that, if he were given his choice, he would prefer to have happened what actually happened. He passed through the other side of life, and now he can continue doing what he wanted to do with all his heart. And the next few weeks we're going to have names added, name after name of people who are going to be brought out of that rubble. And Mychal Judge is going to be on the other side of death . . . to greet them.

GEORGE TAKEI
1937—PRESENT

tl;dr Social-media sensation Takei (rhymes with
"gay," not "bi") tests—and exceeds—the limits
of the American Dream

G eorge was used to seeing himself on television, particularly as the honest and honorable Lieutenant Sulu on *Star Trek*. But watching the protesters on TV that September night in 2005, he knew there was a more important role for him to play. It was a role he'd been subconsciously preparing for his entire life.

George looked over at the man beside him on the couch, his secret partner of eighteen years, as the ticker rolled across the screen: "Schwarzenegger Vetoes California Gay Marriage Bill." It was a slap in the face after Ah-nold campaigned saying he had gay friends and would be friendly to gay issues. The state legislature had passed marriage equality, yet the actor-turned-politician unilaterally decided he wouldn't honor their vote. Same-sex sex had been decriminalized nationally in the United States only two years earlier, and the push for marriage equality was meeting resistance at every turn.

As George watched the video feed of protesters pour-ing out into the LA streets, he remembered that feeling from decades ago when he had marched with Martin Luther King Jr. To march freely, demanding equality for all, bravely parading past counterprotesters and police, knowing that justice was on your side: that was what it meant to be American, to be alive.

George was also taking stock of his own role in the fight for human rights. He'd lived closeted all these years, but he belonged out on that street. At sixty-eight years old, George decided he could no longer be a silent bystander. Schwarzenegger's veto set his blood boiling. It was time to risk everything he had built and bring all the pieces of his identity into the open. That night, George and his beloved, Brad, planned their public coming out.

Number 12832-C

The government had hurt George—and his sense of identity—before. When he was only four years old, an American citizen born and living in LA, soldiers came for his family with guns. Let's repeat that: SOLDIERS with GUNS came for George and his AMERICAN family in the middle of LOS ANGELES. They forced the Takeis to leave everything behind: their home, their money, their possessions. George and his parents, brother, and sister were given numbered ID tags and crowded onto trains with hard wooden seats alongside other Japanese Americans, under the orders of President Franklin D. Roosevelt.

There were no charges, no trial; like the other citizens who were rounded up and forced into internment camps, George's only crime was looking kinda like the Japanese soldiers who had recently bombed Pearl Harbor in 1941. When the United States declared war on Japan in World War II, the government became nervous about the high concentration of people of Japanese descent living on the West Coast and felt the only way to protect national security was to imprison all of them until the war was over. So under an executive order from the White House, they did just that. They *actually imprisoned* more than one hundred thousand people.

George's train took him through hundreds of miles of desert before arriving at the swamps of Arkansas. His parents sold the journey as an adventure for the three kids, a "long vacation in the country." George and his family spent the next three years in detention camps, eating crappy food at the cafeteria, being followed by a spotlight from a sentry tower when they went to use the communal bathroom at night, and reciting the Pledge of Allegiance to a flag waving ever so ironically in front of a barbed-wire fence. The injustice of it all was lost on little George, who adapted to whatever life put in front of him at the time without understanding the bigger picture.

Getting out of the internment camp at the end of World War II in 1945 was scarier than being in it. Anti-Japanese-American frenzy was at an all-time high. With no home to return to, the Takeis were forced to start from scratch after being dropped off by train at the same station they had been taken from years earlier. They lived on Skid Row, then the barrio of East LA. Only other Asians would hire them, so George's dad started as a dishwasher in a Chinese restaurant. Eventually the Takeis climbed back up the economic ladder, and George and his siblings were able to go to college.

Being Japanese American brought enough discrimination into George's life, so he didn't want to stand out as different in any other way. He tried to blend in at school, but fate had other plans. A personal history of persecution had taught George the value of being the same—but he was different, and no amount of lying to himself would change that.

Playing the Part

George made an important discovery about his identity during his freshman year of college in San Francisco—but it's not the typical coed revelation you might expect. Despite his best effort to walk the traditional line his parents envisioned for him by majoring in architecture, George knew his heart was elsewhere. He realized he wanted to be an actor.

George came out to his dad about his true ambitions; Mr. Takei took the news better than George expected, though he wasn't thrilled at the idea of such an unstable career path for his son. Despite the limited on-screen roles for Asian Americans in the 1950s and '60s, George started booking work right away.

George had already acted in movies with the likes of Frank Sinatra, but landing *Star Trek* in 1965 was a major break. A regular TV show meant steady employment. Even more special, the role of Sulu boldly took Asian Americans where they had never gone before. The USS *Enterprise* was a metaphor for

"Starship Earth," and the crew was multiracial at a time when integration was controversial. Instead of a soldier or a servant, George was playing a pilot, a respected member of an elite team. Three TV seasons and six movies later, George was a true Trekkie hero . . . but still completely closeted.

The Final Frontier

George had known he felt about boys the way he was "supposed" to feel about girls from an early age. He also knew he had to keep his sexuality hidden if he wanted to continue acting. For much of George's lifetime, being gay was completely illegal in America and considered perverse by a majority of his fellow citizens (fellow citizens who had also allowed internment camps on American soil). Before the 2010s, George would have risked not only his acting career but possible jail time and other serious consequences for coming out.

George met Brad in a running group in the eighties, and both men understood the need to stay in the closet. They participated in marches during the AIDS epidemic but said they were just straight allies of the cause. George even went so far as to jokingly ask Howard Stern if he was "homo" when the host said he found George's deep voice attractive on a 1990 episode of Stern's radio show. When Howard asked him the same question back, George replied "Oh, no, no, no, no, no."

Fifteen years later, California was poised to become the second state in the United States to experience marriage equality when Schwarzenegger dashed that dream. It was the tipping point for George and Brad. For the next three years, following George's coming-out interview with *Frontiers* magazine, the two of them appeared on talk show after talk show, debating with homophobes and defending their relationship. The battle was punctuated with a moment of joy when the couple married during the brief window in 2008 when doing so was possible in California, before a public vote narrowly took away that right . . . until a 2013 state supreme court ruling secured marriage equality for good.

On the day Brad Altman became Brad Takei, he said in his vows: "Over the more than twenty-one years we have been together, I have called you many things . . . : my life partner, my significant other, my longtime companion, my lover. . . . Beginning today, a dream comes true for me. I can add 'my husband' to the list of things I call you." The two men in matching white tuxedos beamed with joy as *Star Trek* costars stood beside them as best man and best lady. George was whole— a gay man, a Japanese American, a social justice activist for those communities and others—not holding back any piece of himself. Today, George remains a fearlessly outspoken public figure, using his platform both to make people laugh and to challenge injustice everywhere.

LOOKING BACK, MOVING FORWARD

What is remarkable, and at once unsurprising, is that all twenty-three of these queer people lived with such vivid, incandescent variety. Diversity is one of the only constants that queerness has always had, and our unique individuals are connected precisely because they diverged from what society expected.

Queer people are as much a real, interconnected part of the story of our world as everyone else we learn about in school. It matters that we say and demonstrate how queerness itself is as old as time, because people still find it counterintuitive to their conceptions of history. Think about everyone we covered in this book: some were total opposites who wouldn't have considered themselves part of the same community, while others we can picture being best friends if time-and-space travel were possible. Can you imagine a conversation between Kristina and Juana, both known as highly educated women though neither of them felt entirely like a woman? Or Elagabalus and Abraham disagreeing about how to balance governing a nation with having a personal life? Meanwhile, Jeanne, Bayard, and Sylvia would have had a serious debate about how to lead a revolution. Josef didn't know that Alan was working on the other side of the English Channel to shorten his stay in Flossenbürg, and we'll never know if Harvey would have won his City Hall seat if José hadn't run for it years before. They all owe a debt to one another, and we owe a debt to all of them.

But even with so much trailblazing up until this point in history, there's no doubt that the queer community still has a lot of fighting to do. Fear of rejection, physical violence, execution, conversion therapy, and more still haunt millions of queer people's daily lives. In countries like the United States and the United Kingdom, transgender people and other groups marginalized within the queer community are still fighting for basic rights and safety. And coming out remains a scary process even when you're in a safe environment. Thinking about the amount of progress yet to be accomplished can be overwhelming, but when we put it in the context of *all of time*, we see that we've been going in the right direction for hundreds of years and that queer people have always accomplished the unimaginable. We know achieving queer rights is possible because history shows us how it's been done before. And we know that we will adapt to survive and thrive, no matter what happens around us.

Ultimately, the lesson from our twenty-three incredible individuals is that there is no wrong way to be queer. You can be low-key; you can be fabulous; you can exclusively wear shirts with unnecessarily convoluted Judith Butler quotes in very small fonts. You can crusade publicly for equality or pursue your passions while keeping your business your own. All these stories are about people who brought originality, courage, and love to their work—whatever that work was, whatever way they set themselves to it. And as we see in all these transformative lives, and from the effect reading about them has on us today, however you want to live is valid and important—because the mere fact of you, living, makes the world more radiant.

Live bravely.

GLOSSARY

Asexual

Not experiencing sexual attraction, or experiencing sexual attraction very rarely. "Ace" for short. Note that this is not the same as "aromantic," which refers to a person who does not experience (or rarely experiences) romantic attraction. Like many of the orientations defined below, both exist on a spectrum. Kristina Vasa and Eleanor Roosevelt might have identified as asexual today.

Bisexual

Attracted to members of the same gender and also to

people of other genders. The attraction is not necessarily split evenly between men and women and does not have to be restricted to only men and women. "Bi" for short. The term in its modern use first showed up in 1892 in the German text *Psychopathia Sexualis*. Many people from this book would find it the closest term for them today, possibly including Kristina Vasa, Ma Rainey, Frida Kahlo, and Sylvia Rivera.

Cisgender

A person whose gender identity matches up with the biological sex they were assigned at birth. Example: when the doctor says "It's a boy!" and then the child grows up to feel like a man inside. The opposite of transgender. Abraham Lincoln, Eleanor Roosevelt, Josef Kohout, and Harvey Milk are likely some examples of cisgender people.

Conversion Therapy

Any type of therapy that tries to "cure" or change a queer person into a straight and or cisgender person. There is no therapy that achieves this, and its legality is in limbo. Measures in past decades were more extreme, such as electroconvulsive ("shock") therapy, but today in the United States it usually consists of psychological counseling.

Cross-Dressing; Cross-Dresser

Wearing clothes of the gender or sex different from the one you were assigned at birth, like Jeanne d'Arc. Before the word "transgender" existed, this word was often the substitute. Today they are different: a transgender woman dressing as a woman is not cross-dressing because she is dressing as her gender.

Gay

Attracted exclusively to members of the same sex or gender, such as Glenn Burke and George Takei. Traditionally refers to men attracted to men but can also refer to women attracted to women. Sometimes still used as an umbrella term for all nonstraight sexual identities.

Gender; Gender Identity

How someone identifies internally (examples: man, woman, genderqueer, etc.). Different from "sex," which is biologically assigned (examples: male, female, intersex, etc.) and refers to physical and genetic characteristics like genitalia and chromosomes.

Gender Dysphoria

Medical diagnosis for a person whose gender at birth isn't the same as the one they identify with. In 2013 this term replaced "gender identity disorder" in the United States's *Diagnostic and Statistical Manual of Mental Disorders* (DSM) in an effort to destigmatize being trans as "disordered" or "mentally ill." However, "gender dysphoria" is culturally used to refer to the distress resulting from one's gender identity not matching their perceived gender or assigned sex.

Genderqueer

A gender identity of people who do not identify as either male or female. The term showed up in the 1990s. It can also be used as an umbrella term for all kinds of nonbinary gender identities. Kristina Vasa and Mercedes de Acosta might identify under this category if they were alive today.

Heterosexual; Heterosexuality

Exclusively attracted to members of a different sex or gender. Simply: straight, not gay. The term "heterosexuality" didn't appear in the dictionary until 1923; it was invented as the opposite to "homosexuality," which was coined in the 1860s.

Homosexual; Homosexuality

Exclusively attracted to members of the same sex or gender, like Josef Kohout or Harvey Milk. Once the primary word to describe gay people, today it can have a stigmatizing connotation. The term first publicly appeared in a German pamphlet in 1869.

Intersex

Someone whose combination of physical characteristics (chromosomes, hormones, internal and external reproductive organs, etc.) isn't exclusively male or female. Before "intersex," the term was "hermaphrodite," which is now often considered a slur. Lili Elbe was born with both testes and ovaries, so she was intersex.

Intimate Friendship

A type of relationship in the eighteenth, nineteenth, and early twentieth centuries that involved intimacy between two members of the same sex or gender at a greater level than a regular friendship—for example, living as life partners and professing love for each other. This is the type of relationship that Abraham Lincoln had with Joshua Speed and that Eleanor Roosevelt had with Lorena Hickok.

Lesbian

A woman who is exclusively attracted to other women. Del Martin identified and Phyllis Lyon identifies as lesbian.

LGBTQ

Abbreviation for lesbian, gay, bisexual, transgender, and queer or questioning. Questioning refers to people who are currently figuring out their sexual and gender identities. LGBT and GLBT are also common abbreviations. You may see other additions after LGBT: "I" (intersex), "2S" (Two-Spirit), "A" (asexual or ally), and more. As the acronym has grown in length ("LGBTTIQQ2SAA," for example, which still leaves out many identities), the popularity of "queer" as a catch-all for all nonheterosexual noncisgender identities has grown as well.

Nonbinary

Similar to "genderqueer," an umbrella term for gender identities that aren't exclusively male or female.

Queen; Drag Queen

"Drag queen" and "queen" were commonly used along with "cross-dresser" before the word "transgender" existed to refer to transgender women. Today this is not a term that would be used for a transgender woman. "Drag queen" still exists as a term for someone like José Sarria, a man who dresses as a woman for performance—but not to express a consistent female gender identity.

Queer

Often used today as an umbrella term for everyone who isn't heterosexual or cisgender (also often only refers to nonheterosexuals, so you might say "queer and trans" to be inclusive). Reclaimed in the 1990s from being an antigay slur. Still a controversial term that can be seen as derogatory. In this book we use it to mean any identity not completely fitting the modern concepts of heterosexual or cisgender, even if the person did not self-identify as "queer" or if sexual identity labels did not exist at all during that person's time.

Sex Reassignment Surgery

Medical term for the surgeries that physically change someone's anatomy from male to female or female to male, such as creating or removing breasts, a penis, or a vagina. "Gender affirmation surgery" is often a better choice of term today. Not all transgender people want to undergo surgical procedures to change their sex—no matter what bodies they have, their gender identity is who they are.

Sodomy; Sodomite

Anal or oral sex. In the Middle Ages, before the word "homosexuality" existed, this was the predominant term for talking about homosexual behavior. It is still a crime in many countries today. A "sodomite" is a person who commits sodomy.

They/Them/Their

One of many sets of gender-neutral singular pronouns used as an alternative to she/her/her or he/him/his.

Transgender

A person whose gender identity does not match up with the biological sex they were assigned at birth. Example: when the doctor says "It's a boy!" and then the child grows up to feel like a woman inside. An umbrella term encompassing many identities. "Trans" for short. "Transgender" came into use in the 1970s.

Transsexual

A term under the transgender umbrella referring specifically to those who wish to make, are going through, or have already undergone a physical transition from one sex to another with hormones and/or gender affirmation surgery (sex reassignment surgery). This term was used more broadly before "transgender" was popularized. Renée Richards is an example of a transsexual person.

Transvestite

Essentially a synonym for cross-dresser.

Two-Spirit

A Native (or American Indian) term chosen in 1990 to cover all the dozens of First Nations' identities involving both male and female appearing in one person.

Online resources are best equipped to reflect the ever-changing language of queerness. Let Google be your friend!

LEARN MORE

For additional information on the featured historymakers and more, visit:

www.sarahprager.com/queerthere

For a comprehensive listing of websites, apps, social media projects, and other online resources for learning queer history, visit:

www.quistapp.com/online-resources

BIBLIOGRAPHY & NOTES

Introduction

Boswell, John. *Christianity, Social Tolerance, and Homosexuality: Gay People in Western Europe from the Beginning of the Christian Era to the Fourteenth Century.* Chicago: University of Chicago Press, 1980.

Brabant, Malcolm. "Lesbos Islanders Dispute Gay Name." BBC News. May 1, 2008. http://news.bbc.co.uk/2/hi /europe/7376919.stm.

Centers for Disease Control and Prevention. "HIV and AIDS— United States, 1981–2000." https://www.cdc.gov/mmwr /preview/mmwrhtml/mm5021a2.htm.

Crompton, Louis. *Homosexuality & Civilization.* Cambridge,

MA: Belknap, 2003.

Gay & Lesbian Kingdom. "History." Accessed June 15, 2016. http://gaykingdom.info/history.htm.

———. "Stamps." Accessed June 15, 2016. http://gaykingdom .info/stamps.htm.

Hayward, Claire. "Queer Terminology: LGBTQ Histories and the Semantics of Sexuality." Notches (blog). June 9, 2016. http://notchesblog.com/2016/06/09/queer-terminology -lgbtq-histories-and-the-semantics-of-sexuality/.

Murray, Stephen O., and Will Roscoe. *Islamic Homosexualities: Culture, History, and Literature.* New York: New York University Press, 1997.

———, eds. *Boy-Wives and Female Husbands: Studies in African Homosexualities.* New York: Palgrave, 1998.

Norton, Rictor. "Some Thoughts on . . . The History of the Word 'Gay' and Other Queerwords." Essays by Rictor Norton. Accessed June 15, 2016. http://rictornorton.co.uk /though23.htm.

Roscoe, Will. *Changing Ones: Third and Fourth Genders in Native North America.* New York: St. Martin's Press, 1998.

Stern, Keith. *Queers in History: The Comprehensive Encyclopedia of Historical Gays, Lesbians, Bisexuals, and Transgenders.* Dallas, TX: BenBella Books, 2009.

Stryker, Susan. *Transgender History.* Berkeley, CA: Seal Press, 2008.

Tomilson, Maurice. "Caleb Orozco Sets a Valuable Caribbean
Precedent." Erasing 76 Crimes (blog). Accessed August 18,
2016. https://76crimes.com/2016/08/16/caleb-orozco-sets
-a-valuable-caribbean-precedent.

To say this overview is the short, simplified version of
queer history is an understatement. While striving to profile
a diverse selection of identities, the author found that there
was not enough source material available to tell the stories of
many from other parts of the world in the required detail, due
to a lack of records. For various non-Western profiles we considered, the records were either never written, were destroyed,
or never allowed to be written at all (as was the case for slaves
of pan-African descent in the Americas). Another factor is
the author's lack of access to existing oral or written histories
abroad or in other languages. There is *so much more* to learn
out there! A list of more people who could have had their own
chapters can be found at www.sarahprager.com/queerthere.

Elagabalus

Herodian. *Herodian* 5.5. 2007. www.livius.org/sources/content
/herodian-s-roman-history/herodian-5.5/?.
———. *Herodian* 5.8. 2007. www.livius.org/sources/content
/herodian-s-roman-history/herodian-5.8/?.

Hersch, Karen K. *The Roman Wedding: Ritual and Meaning in Antiquity*. New York: Cambridge University Press, 2010.

Icks, Martjin. *The Crimes of Elagabalus: The Life and Legacy of Rome's Decadent Boy Emperor*. London: I. B. Tauris, 2013.

Mijatovic, Alexis. "A Brief Biography of Elagabalus: The Transgender Ruler of Rome." Accessed May 5, 2016. http://outhistory.org/exhibits/show/tgi-bios/elagabalus.

Thayer, Bill, ed. *Historia Augusta*. Accessed May 13, 2016. http://penelope.uchicago.edu/Thayer/E/Roman/Texts /Historia_Augusta/Elagabalus/1*.html.

———. *Roman History by Cassius Dio: Epitome of Book LXXIX*. Accessed May 13, 2016. http://penelope.uchicago.edu /Thayer/E/Roman/Texts/Cassius_Dio/79*.html.

———. *Roman History by Cassius Dio: Epitome of Book LXXX*. Accessed May 13, 2016. http://penelope.uchicago.edu/ Thayer/E/Roman/Texts/Cassius_Dio/80*.html.

Cassius Dio uses male pronouns to refer to Elagabalus, as do essentially all books about her. Female pronouns were chosen as the most appropriate for this individual based on her own statements of self-identification.

"My Lord Emperor, hail" and "Call me not Lord, for I am a lady": Thayer, *Roman History by Cassius Dio: Epitome of Book LXXX*.

Jeanne D'Arc (Joan of Arc)

Brooks, Polly Schoyer. *Beyond the Myth: The Story of Joan of Arc.* New York: J. B. Lippincott, 1990.

Castor, Helen. *Joan of Arc: A History.* New York: HarperCollins, 2015.

Crane, Susan. "Clothing and Gender Definition: Joan of Arc." *Journal of Medieval and Early Modern Studies* 26, no. 2 (Spring 1996): 297–320.

Sackville-West, Vita. *Saint Joan of Arc.* Garden City, NY: Doubleday, Doran & Company, 1936.

Sanguinetti, Emilia Philomena. *Joan of Arc: Her Trial Transcripts.* Dallas, TX: Little Flower, 2015.

All cited references use the Anglicized "Joan" to refer to Jeanne. "Jeanne" is the French spelling used by Jeanne and her contemporaries.

"God's will is done": Castor, 127.
"In her": Sanguinetti, 80.

Kristina Vasa (Christina of Sweden)

Buckley, Veronica. *Christina Queen of Sweden: The Restless Life of a European Eccentric.* New York: Harper Perennial, 2004.

Christina, Queen of Sweden. *Maxims of a Queen, Christina of Sweden (1626–89)*. Una Birch, transl. Forgotten Books, 2012.

Goldsmith, Margaret. *Christina of Sweden: A Psychological Biography*. New York: Doubleday, Doran & Company, 1933.

Herbermann, Charles George, ed. *The Catholic Encyclopedia: An International Work of Reference on the Constitution, Doctrine, Discipline, and History of the Catholic Church*. Vol. 3. New York: Encyclopedia Press, 1908.

Stolpe, Sven. *Christina of Sweden*. Edited by Sir Alec Randall. New York: Macmillan, 1966.

Woodhead, Henry. *Memoirs of Christina, Queen of Sweden*. 2 vols. London: Hurst and Blackett, 1863.

All cited references use female pronouns to refer to Kristina. Gender-neutral pronouns were chosen as the most appropriate for this individual because their gender identity is unclear.

All cited references use the Anglicized "Christina" to refer to Kristina. "Kristina" is the Swedish spelling used by Kristina and their contemporaries.

"I hope this girl . . .": Woodhead, Vol. 1, 11–12.
"As a young girl . . .": Buckley, 55.

"It is almost impossible . . .": Woodhead, Vol. 1, 95.

"Tenderness": Woodhead, Vol. 2, 205.

"In whatever part of the world . . .": Woodhead, Vol. 2, 204.

"My love is so strong . . .": Woodhead, Vol. 1, 201.

"Could not bear . . .": Buckley, 72.

"Felt such a repulsion . . .": Goldsmith, 72–73.

"I am free at last!": Woodhead, Vol. 2, 169.

Juana Inés de la Cruz

Calvo, Hortensia, and Beatriz Colombi, eds. *Cartas De Lysi: La mecenas de sor Juana Inés de la Cruz en correspondencia inédita.* Madrid: IberoamericanaVervuert, 2015.

de la Cruz, Sor Juana Inés. "Selected Works." Isle of Lesbos. Translated by Alan S. Trueblood. Accessed June 17, 2016. www.sappho.com/poetry/j_ines.html.

———. *Sor Juana's Love Poems.* Joan Larkin and Jaime Manrique, transl. Madison, Wisc.: University of Wisconsin Press, 1997.

Paz, Octavio. *Sor Juana, or, The Traps of Faith.* Translated by Margaret Sayers Peden. Cambridge, MA: Belknap, 1988.

Rupp, Leila. *Sapphistries: A Global History of Love between Women.* New York: New York University Press, 2009.

Wesley Ministry Network. "Reading for Session 4. Juana Inés

de la Cruz: Respuesta a Sor Filotea de la Cruz (1690)."
Women Speak of God: Participant's Guide. Accessed June
7, 2016. www.wesleyministrynetwork.com/wsog/sample
_lesson.pdf.

Opening poem: Rupp, 76–77.
"Loving you is a crime . . .": de la Cruz.
"That you're a woman . . .": de la Cruz.
"Who merely by virtue of being men . . .": Wesley Ministry
Network.
"From all I did not say . . .": Paz, 223.

Abraham Lincoln

Flynt, Larry, and David Eisenbach. *One Nation under Sex: How
the Private Lives of Presidents, First Ladies and Their Lovers
Changed the Course of American History.* New York: Palgrave
Macmillan, 2011.

Goodheart, Adam. "The Bedfellows' Reunion." *New York Times,*
November 25, 2010. http://opinionator.blogs.nytimes
.com/2010/11/25/the-bedfellows-reunion/?_r=0.

Johnson, Martin P. "Did Abraham Lincoln Sleep with His
Bodyguard? Another Look at the Evidence." *Journal of the
Abraham Lincoln Association,* 27, no. 2 (Summer 2006): 42–55.

Katz, Jonathan Ned. *Love Stories: Sex between Men before Homosexuality.* Chicago: University of Chicago Press, 2001.

Speed, Joshua Fry. *Reminiscences of Abraham Lincoln and Notes of a Visit to California: Two Lectures.* Louisville, KY: John P. Morton, 1884.

Stozier, Charles B. *Your Friend Forever, A. Lincoln: The Enduring Friendship of Abraham Lincoln and Joshua Speed.* New York: Columbia University Press, 2005.

Tripp, C. A. *The Intimate World of Abraham Lincoln.* New York: Free Press, 2005.

Vidal, Gore. "Was Lincoln Bisexual?" *Vanity Fair,* January 2005. www.vanityfair.com/news/2005/01/lincoln200501.

"I am now the most miserable man living": Flynt, 58.

"I have a large room . . .": Speed, 22.

"No two men were ever more intimate": Flynt, 57.

"Loved this man . . .": Flynt, 57.

"Indescribably horrible": Tripp, 150.

"Far happier than . . .": Katz, 23.

"Lincoln looked and acted . . .": Tripp, 157.

"Tish says . . .": Tripp, 1.

"In Mrs. Lincoln's absence . . .": Tripp, 3.

"Speed and Lincoln poured . . .": Tripp, 145.

Albert Cashier

Benck, Amy. "Albert D. J. Cashier: Woman Warrior, Insane Civil War Veteran, or Transman?" Accessed May 5, 2016. http://outhistory.org/exhibits/show/tgi-bios/albert -cashier.

Blanton, DeAnne, and Lauren M. Cook. *They Fought Like Demons: Women Soldiers in the American Civil War.* Baton Rouge: Louisiana State University Press, 2002.

Clausius, Gerhard P. "The Little Soldier of the 95th: Albert D. J. Cashier." *Journal of the Illinois State Historical Society (1908– 1984),* 51, no. 4 (1958): 380–87.

Lawson, Don. *Also Known as Albert D. J. Cashier: The Jennie Hodgers Story, or How One Young Irish Girl Joined the Union Army during the Civil War.* Chicago: Compass Rose Cultural Crossroads, 2005.

Paul, Linda. "In Civil War, Woman Fought Like a Man for Freedom." All Things Considered. May 24, 2009. www.npr.org/templates/story/story.php?storyId=104452266.

US National Park Service. "Jennie Hodgers, aka Private Albert Cashier." Accessed May 5, 2016. https://www.nps.gov /articles/Jennie-hodgers-aka-private-albert-cashier.htm.

Most cited references use female pronouns and the name Jennie Hodgers to refer to Albert. Male pronouns and the name

Albert Cashier were chosen as the most appropriate for this individual because of their life living as male. The decision to mention Albert's birth name at all in this chapter was due to historical storytelling necessity.

"He was a right feisty . . .": Lawson, 202.

"Those colors should be flying free!": Lawson, 223.

"He might be the littlest . . .": Lawson, 224.

Gertrude "Ma" Rainey

Brown, Sterling A. "Ma Rainey." *AfroPoets Famous Writers.* Accessed October 29, 2015. www.afropoets.net /sterlingbrown8.html.

Davis, Angela Y. *Blues Legacies and Black Feminism: Gertrude "Ma" Rainey, Bessie Smith, and Billie Holiday.* New York: Pantheon Books, 1998.

Davis, Francis. *The History of the Blues: The Roots, the Music, the People from Charley Patton to Robert Cray.* New York: Hyperion, 1995.

Katz, Jonathan Ned. "Ma Rainey's 'Prove It on Me Blues,'" 1928. Accessed November 10, 2015. http://outhistory.org /exhibits/show/rainey/rainey2.

McGasko, Joe. "The Mother and the Empress: Ma Rainey and Bessie Smith." May 15, 2015. www.biography.com/news

/bessie-smith-ma-rainey-biography.

Memphis Minnie. "Ma Rainey." Accessed October 29, 2015. www.oldielyrics.com/lyrics/memphis_minnie/ma_rainey .html.

Oakley, Giles. *The Devil's Music: A History of the Blues.* New York: Taplinger, 1977.

"Prove It on Me Blues" lyrics: Davis, 1998, 39–40.

"People it sure look lonesome . . .": Memphis Minnie.

Lili Elbe

Hoyer, Niels. *Man into Woman.* London: Jarrolds Publishers, 1933.

Meyerowitz, Joanne. *How Sex Changed: A History of Transsexuality.* Cambridge, MA: Harvard University Press, 2002.

Rohrer, Megan. "Surgery: From Top to Bottom." Accessed April 27, 2016. http://outhistory.org/exhibits/show /man-i-fest/exhibit/surgery.

The way Lili's life and transition are described is based on her own detailed account of it in Hoyer, including the times male pronouns and the name Einar Wegener are used.

"You look just as if . . .": Hoyer, 64.

"You were certainly a girl . . .": Hoyer, 65.

"I understand you . . .": Hoyer, 27.

"It may be said that . . .": Hoyer, 278.

Frida Kahlo

Collins, Amy Fine. "Diary of a Mad Artist." *Vanity Fair,*
    September 3, 2013. www.vanityfair.com/culture/1995/09
    /frida-kahlo-diego-rivera-art-diary.

Herrera, Hayden. *Frida: A Biography of Frida Kahlo.* New York:
    Harper & Row, 1983.

History Chicks, The. "Episode 42: Frida Kahlo." Podcast audio,
    September 9, 2015. http://thehistorychicks.com
    /episode-42-frida-kahlo-2.

"I didn't come here for fun . . .": Herrera, 88.

"I did not know it then . . .": Herrera, 89.

"Woman chaser": Herrera, 87.

"I see you're interested in my daughter . . ." conversation:
Herrera, 89.

"An elephant and a dove": Herrera, 99.

"Make love . . .": Herrera, 199.

Mercedes de Acosta

Cohen, Lisa. *All We Know: Three Lives*. New York: Farrar, Straus and Giroux, 2012.

Schanke, Robert A. *"That Furious Lesbian": The Story of Mercedes de Acosta*. Carbondale: Southern Illinois University Press, 2003.

Vickers, Hugo. *Loving Garbo: The Story of Greta Garbo, Cecil Beaton, and Mercedes de Acosta*. New York: Random House, 1994.

The decision to use female pronouns for Mercedes de Acosta was made because she used them for herself throughout her life after childhood.

Opening scene: Vickers, 9–10.

"The tragedy": Vickers, 9.

"In that one brief second . . .": Vickers, 10.

"I am not a boy . . .": Cohen, 161.

"I do not understand . . .": Vickers, 10.

Truman Capote anecdote: Vickers, 12.

"Pour my love into you": Vickers, 76.

"I can get any woman . . .": Vickers, 12.

"I was walking on flowers . . .": Schanke, 114.

"Golden One": Vickers, 61.

"In Europe it doesn't matter . . .": Vickers, 58.

"I bought it for you in Berlin": Vickers, 27.

"You and me. There is no other way": Schanke, 150.

Eleanor Roosevelt

Burns, Ken. *The Roosevelts: An Intimate History.* PBS, 2014.

Cook, Blanche Wiesen. *Eleanor Roosevelt: Vol. I, 1884–1933.* New York: Viking Penguin, 1992.

Hickok, Lorena. *Reluctant First Lady: An Intimate Story of Eleanor Roosevelt's Early Public Life.* New York: Dodd, Mead, 1962.

Lash, Joseph P. *Love, Eleanor: Eleanor Roosevelt and her Friends.* New York: Doubleday, 1982.

Potter, Claire Bond. "Public Figures, Private Lives: Eleanor Roosevelt, J. Edgar Hoover, and a Queer Political History." In *Understanding and Teaching U.S. Lesbian, Gay, Bisexual, and Transgender History.* Edited by Leila J. and Susan K. Freeman Rupp, 199–212. Madison: University of Wisconsin Press, 2014.

Pottker, Jan. *Sara and Eleanor: The Story of Sara Delano Roosevelt and Her Daughter-in-Law, Eleanor Roosevelt.* New York: St. Martin's Press, 2004.

Streitmatter, Rodger, ed. *Empty without You: The Intimate Letters of Eleanor Roosevelt and Lorena Hickok.* New York: Free Press, 1998.

US Department of Health, Education, and Welfare. "100 Years of Marriage and Divorce Statistics United States, 1867–1967." Rockville, MD, 1973.

"Ordeal to be born": Pottker, 116.
"Love nest": Streitmatter, xix.
"Your mother wasn't . . .": Streitmatter, xxii.
Letter excerpts: Streitmatter.
"I love you with all my heart": Streitmatter, 225.

Bayard Rustin

D'Emilio, John. *Lost Prophet: The Life and Times of Bayard Rustin*. Chicago: University of Chicago Press, 2004.
Drayton, Robert. "The Personal Life of Bayard Rustin." *OUT*. January 18, 2016. www.out.com/news-opinion/2013/08/28/bayard-rustin-walter-naegle-partner-gay-civil-rights-activist-march-washington.

Opening scene: D'Emilio, 46.
"This man impresses me . . .": D'Emilio, 100.
"Being black, being homosexual . . .": Drayton.

Alan Turing

Hodges, Andrew. *Alan Turing: The Enigma*. Princeton, NJ: Princeton University Press, 1983.

"He was a real convert . . .": Hodges, 575.

Josef Kohout

Heger, Heinz. *The Men with the Pink Triangle*. Boston: Alyson Publications, 1980.

Setterington, Ken. *Branded by the Pink Triangle*. Toronto: Second Story, 2013.

United States Holocaust Memorial Museum. "Documenting Nazi Persecution of Gays: The Josef Kohout/Wilhelm Kroepfl Collection." Accessed April 29, 2016. https://www.ushmm.org/information/exhibitions/curators-corner/documenting-nazi-persecution-of-gays-the-josef-kohout-wilhelm-kroepfl-collection.

———. "Paragraph 175." Accessed April 28, 2016. https://www.ushmm.org/learn/students/learning-materials-and-resources/homosexuals-victims-of-the-nazi-era/paragraph-175.

Opening scene: Heger, 71.

"It's your life and you must live it . . .": Heger, 20.

"You are a queer . . .": Heger, 23.

"In eternal love and deepest affection": Heger, 23.

"A male who commits lewd . . .": United States Holocaust Memorial Museum, Paragraph 175.

"You want to come with me?": Heger, 48.

"God protect our son!": Heger, 22.

José Sarria

Gorman, Michael R. *The Empress Is a Man: Stories from the Life of José Sarria*. Binghamton, NY: Harrington Park, 1998.

Imperial Council of San Francisco. "Founder." Accessed May 3, 2016. www.imperialcouncilsf.org/founder.html.

International Court System, The. "50 Years of Noble Deeds." Accessed May 4, 2016. www.impcourt.org/8-about-us/213 -about-us-2.

Sarria, José, interview by Paul Gabriel. San Francisco: GLBT Historical Society, September 15, 1996.

José used male pronouns when out of drag and female pronouns when in drag, following traditional etiquette.

Exchange starting with "What's the charge, officer?": Gorman, 179–180.

"United we stand . . .": Gorman, 219.

"José was the first person . . .": Gorman, 241.

"I proved my point . . .": Gorman, 207.

Del Martin & Phyllis Lyon

Biren, Joan E. *No Secret Anymore*. San Francisco, CA: Frameline Distribution, 2007. Available on streaming online video.

Gallo, Marcia M. *Different Daughters: A History of the Daughters of Bilitis and the Rise of the Lesbian Rights Movement*. New York: Carroll & Graf, 2006.

Johnson, Dianna Lee. "A Narrative Life Story of Activist Phyllis Lyon and Her Reflections on a Life with Del Martin." Master's thesis, Grand Valley State University, 2012. http://scholarworks.gvsu.edu/cgi/viewcontent .cgi?article=1021&context=theses.

Lagos, Marisa, Rachel Gordon, Chris Heredia, and Jill Tucker. "Same-Sex Weddings Start with Union of Elderly San Francisco Couple." *San Francisco Chronicle*, June 17, 2008. www.sfgate.com/news/article/Same-sex-weddings-start -with-union-of-elderly-San-3208657.php.

Louÿs, Pierre. "Counsels." Translated by Alvah C. Bessie.

Accessed June 20, 2016. www.sacred-texts.com/cla/sob
/index.htm.

"So I did": Biren.
"Why worry about it": Biren.
"Titles of editor . . .": Johnson, 56.
"Something to do with love": Biren.
"Only women know the art of love" is a line from "The
Songs of Bilitis": Louÿs.
"AMAZING": Gallo, 1.
"Could have been a society . . .": Gallo, 20.
"If slacks are worn . . .": Gallo, 7.
"Your Name Is Safe!": Gallo, 29.
"Come out of hiding": Gallo, 31.
"What a delicious invitation . . .": Gallo, 31.
"I'm glad as heck that you exist": Gallo, 21.
"When [we] first got together . . .": Lagos.

Sylvia Rivera

Carter, David. *Stonewall: The Riots That Sparked the Gay
Revolution.* New York: St. Martin's, 2004.
Frey, Holly. *Stuff You Missed in History Class.* "Sylvia Rivera."
Podcast audio, October 8, 2014. www.missedinhistory
.com/podcasts/sylvia-rivera/.

History Is a Weapon. "Our Armies Are Rising and We Are
Getting Stronger." Accessed April 30, 2016.
www.historyisaweapon.com/defcon1
/riverarisingandstronger.html.

National Parks Conservation Association. "A National Park for
Stonewall." Youtube.com/watch?v=9QiigzZCE+Q. August
18, 2016. https://www.npca.org/advocacy/5-a-national
-park-for-stonewall.

New York Times Magazine. "Sylvia Rivera." June 27, 1999. www
.soundportraits.org/in-print/magazine_articles/sylvia
_rivera.

Rivera, Sylvia. "Queens in Exile, the Forgotten Ones." In
GenderQueer: Voices from Beyond the Sexual Binary, edited by
Joan Nestle, Clare Howell, and Riki Wilchins, 67–85. New
York: Alyson Books, 2002.

Sandeen, Autumn. "In Revolution, the Trans Terms Sylvia
Rivera Used." *The Trans Advocate.* April 30, 2014.
www.transadvocate.com/in-revolution-the-trans-terms
-sylvia-rivera-used_n_13623.htm.

*Street Transvestite Action Revolutionaries: Survival, Revolt, and
Queer Antagonist Struggle.* Untorelli Press. Accessed June
17, 2016. www.transadvocate.com/wp-content
/uploads/2014/04/STAR_Pamphlet.pdf.

"Sylvia Rivera—Y'all better quiet down (1973)." Sylvia
speaking at NYC Pride 1973. YouTube video, 4:08. Posted

by Luz Violeta, October 22, 2014.
www.youtube.com/watch?v=9QiigzZCEtQ.

Workers World Service. "Leslie Feinberg interviews Sylvia
Rivera." Accessed June 17, 2016. www.workers.org
/ww/1998/sylvia0702.php.

"Why don't you guys do something!": Carter, 151.

"My God, the revolution . . .": *Street Transvestite Action Revo-lutionaries*, 14.

"Saw the world change . . .": *Street Transvestite Action Revo-lutionaries,* 14.

Marsha P. Johnson, mentioned as Sylvia's friend, is another important founder of the queer rights movement who was just as much a leader as Sylvia.

"I had to fight my way . . .": History Is a Weapon.

"You all tell me . . .": "Sylvia Rivera."

"I feel that both of us being transgendered . . .": *New York Times Magazine.*

Renée Richards

ESPN. *Renée.* Directed by Eric Drath. Owensboro, KY: Team
Marketing, 2011. DVD, 73 minutes.

Richards, Renée, with John Ames. *No Way Renée: The Second Half of my Notorious Life*. New York: Simon & Schuster, 2007.

———. *Second Serve: The Renée Richards Story*. New York: Stein and Day, 1983.

The way Renée's life and transition is described is based on her own detailed account of it in *Second Serve*, *No Way Renée*, and *Renée*, including the times male pronouns and the name Dick Raskind are used.

"Stuff": *Renée*.
"Disgusted": *Renée*.
"So drastic": *Renée*.
"Wanted nothing more . . .": Richards, 2007, 81.
"I'll take a sex test . . .": *Renée*.

Harvey Milk

Richter, Miriam. Re: A New Book Featuring Harvey Milk. E-mail. December 8, 2016.

Shilts, Randy. *The Mayor of Castro Street: The Life and Times of Harvey Milk*. New York: St. Martin's, 1982.

Sward, Susan. "Scott Smith—Harvey Milk Friend." *San Francisco Chronicle*, February 7, 1995.

Telling Pictures Distribution. *The Times of Harvey Milk*. Directed
by Rob Epstein and Richard Schmiechen. San Francisco:
Black Sand Productions, 1984. DVD, 88 minutes.

Weiss, Mike. *Double Play: The San Francisco City Hall Killings*.
Reading, MA: Addison-Wesley, 1984.

"You get the first bullet . . .": Shilts, 223.

"Let me remind you what America is": Shilts, 225.

"Yes, We Are Very Open": Shilts, 65.

"Tell all your friends . . .": Shilts, 162.

"You can stand around . . .": Shilts, 190.

"Change is counterproductive . . .": Shilts, 199.

"Harvey, can I see you . . .": Weiss, 253.

"If a bullet should . . .": Shilts, 372.

Glenn Burke

Branch, John. "Posthumous Recognition: M.L.B to Recognize
Glenn Burke as Baseball's Gay Pioneer." *New York Times*,
July 14, 2014. https://www.nytimes.com/2014/07/15
/sports/baseball/mlb-to-recognize-glenn-burke-as-a-gay
-pioneer-in-baseball.html.

Burke, Glenn, with Erik Sherman. *Out at Home: The True Story
of Glenn Burke, Baseball's First Openly Gay Player*. New York:
Berkley Books, 1995.

Harris, Doug. "The Price Glenn Burke Paid for Coming Out."
    Interview by Kelly McEvers. *All Things Considered*. NPR,
    May 5, 2013. www.npr.org/2013/05/05/181410089/the
    -price-glenn-burke-paid-for-coming-out.

Mooallem, Jon. "The History (and Mystery) of the High
    Five." In *The Best American Sports Writing 2012*, edited
    by Michael Wilbon, 345–52. Boston: Houghton Mifflin
    Harcourt, 2012.

Richmond, Peter. "The Brief Life and Complicated Death of
    Tommy Lasorda's Gay Son." *Deadspin: The Stacks* (blog).
    April 30, 2013. http://thestacks.deadspin.com/the-brief
    -life-and-complicated-death-of-tommy-lasordas
    -485999366.

Spencer, Lyle. "Dodgers of '77 Recall High-Five-Fueled Run to
    Series." MLB.com, October 14, 2013. http://m.mlb.com
    /news/article/62943568.

Watson, Owen. "Glenn Burke's Potential Still Haunts Mike
    Norris." The Hardball Times, July 21, 2015. http://www
    .hardballtimes.com/glenn-burkes-potential-still-haunts
    -mike-norris/

"No faggot . . .": Burke, 68.

"Baseball suicide": Burke, 47.

"Tommy first would have shot us . . .": Burke, 24–25.

"Everybody on this team is married . . .": Burke, 9.

"His hand was up in the air . . .": Mooallem, 347.

"A legacy of two men's hands touching": Mooallem, 350.

"As I reach my final days . . .": Burke, 159.

Mychal Judge

Daly, Michael. *The Book of Mychal: The Surprising Life and Heroic Death of Father Mychal Judge*. New York: St. Martin's, 2008.

Ford, Michael. *Father Mychal Judge: An Authentic American Hero*. New York: Paulist, 2002.

"Mychal, please pray for us." "I always do.": Ford, 7.

"You should go, Padre." "I'm not finished.": Daly, 332.

"Jesus, please end this right now!": Daly, 336.

"Peest": Daly, 5.

"My rival was God": Daly, 127.

"An intrinsic moral evil": Ford, 119.

"They did the same to Jesus": Ford, 121.

"Lit up the White House": Ford, 196.

"There were between two and three hundred . . .": Ford, 196.

George Takei

"From the Vault: George Takei Comes Out." Interview by Alexander Cho, February 21, 2012.

www.frontiersmedia.com/frontiers-blog/2012/02/21
/from-the-vault-george-takei-comes-out.

"George Takei Interview #8: Coming Out Publicly." YouTube
video, 2:52. Posted by DiscoverNikkei, June 18, 2015.
https://youtu.be/MoIdf_qrpAI.

"Howard Stern 1990 George Takei's first appearance."
YouTube video, 1:24. Posted by Rx1922, October 20, 2013.
https://youtu.be/cNBLEPCw1Vo.

Takei, George. "Takei Wedding." Accessed June 7, 2016.
http://georgetakei.com/takei-wedding.

———. *To the Stars: The Autobiography of George Takei, Star Trek's
Mr. Sulu.* New York: Pocket Books, 1995.

"Long vacation in the country": Takei, *To the Stars,* 11–12.

"Oh, no, no, no, no, no": "Howard Stern."

"Over the more than twenty-one years . . .": Takei, "Takei
Wedding."

Glossary

Beredjick, Camille. "DSM-V to Rename Gender Identity
Disorder 'Gender Dysphoria.'" *The Advocate.* July 23, 2012.
http://www.advocate.com/politicstransgender
/2012/07/23/dsm-replaces-gender-identity-disorder
-gender-dysphoria.

Killermann, Sam. "Comprehensive* List of LGBTQ+ Term
    Definitions." It's Pronounced Metrosexual. Accessed
    February 3, 2016. http://itspronouncedmetrosexual
    .com/2013/01/a-comprehensive-list-of-lgbtq-term
    -definitions.

National Center for Lesbian Rights. "#BornPerfect: The Facts
    about Conversion Therapy." Accessed January 25, 2017.
    www.nclrights.org/bornperfect-the-facts-about
    -conversion-therapy.

NativeOUT. "Two Spirit 101." Accessed June 15, 2016. http://
    nativeout.com/twospirit-rc/two-spirit-101.

PFLAG. "PFLAG National Glossary of Terms." Accessed June 9,
    2016. https://www.pflag.org/glossary.

Rictor, Norton. "The Term 'Homosexual.'" A Critique of
    Social Constructionism and Postmodern Queer Theory.
    Accessed June 15, 2016. http://rictornorton.co.uk
    /social14.htm.

Roxie, Marilyn. "Genderqueer History." Genderqueer
    and Non-Binary Identities. Accessed June 15, 2016.
    http://genderqueerid.com/gqhistory.

Williams, Cristan. "Tracking Transgender: The Historical
    Truth." Ehipassiko. July 26, 2012.
    www.cristanwilliams.com/b/2012/03/27/tracking
    -transgender-the-historical-truth.

make it into this book. My vision for *Queer, There, and Everywhere* was much more geographically diverse, but time and research limitations caused me to lose some of the stories I most wanted to tell, like that of Francisco Manicongo. I spent the majority of my time on this book looking in vain for enough detail to make successful chapters out of these people's stories, but the records were too sparse to make strong narratives for this format. I promise them I will continue to tell what we do know of their stories elsewhere and personally remember them.

My whole family—especially my parents, Bev and Rich Prager; my aunt, Mel Julian; and my sister, Alex Scalfano—supported me in so many ways through the process of writing this book. My wife, Liz Prager, played the largest role. I couldn't do any of this without her, and even if I could, I definitely wouldn't want to. Liz, you have supported this crazy quistory career from the moment I randomly started doing research because I felt like it one day in 2013. For always being my first editor, assistant researcher, and cheerleader, this book is yours, too. You never fail to step up when I need you, and I'm so lucky to have you.

And to our sweet baby, Eleanor Hermione, who grew in me as I wrote this book: your moms love you so very much. Thanks for your input with the well-timed kicks. I wish for you Sylvia's strength, Harvey's courage, Del and Phyllis's dedication, and above all, a loving and safe world we'll help to create together.

Prendella for her tireless work on this book. Dillan DiGiovanni, Renée Cafiero, Megan Gendell, Zoë More O'Ferrall, Leila Rupp, Anna Ellis, Desiree Alaniz, Jakob VanLammeren, Adriana Sisko, Jeanne Glynn, Tracy and Matt Barry, Audra Friend, Debbie Richards, Susan Spann, Robbie Samuels, Susan Stryker, Carolyn and Benjamin Oliver, Matt Lyons, Stuart Milk, Miriam Richter, Rebecca Mui, Robyn Ochs, Shane Bitney Crone, Kevin Jennings, Meredith Russo, Sarah McCarry, José Gutierrez, Nancy Moline, Stacey Endress, Mitchell Thorpe, Audrey Diestelkamp, Alison Klapthor, Liz Byer, Roger Cantello, the staff and services of the Wallingford Public Library, and many others helped as well.

I'd also like to thank the entire Quist team. They're all listed at quistapp.com/supporters, but I have to thank Chris Zahka by name here. I will always be grateful for his significant early support that made Quist a reality.

I also acknowledge the individuals profiled in this book. For some, it wasn't possible to gain their permission to tell their stories, but I hope that the fact they lived so openly means they would approve. Each one has inspired me personally, and I am proud to stand on the shoulders of such amazing people. I also owe a huge debt to the researchers and writers who created all the books and resources I consulted that made it possible for me to tell their stories here.

I'd also like to acknowledge the individuals who didn't

QUEER, THERE, AND EVERYWHERE

ACKNOWLEDGMENTS

This book wouldn't exist without Sara Sargent, my editor at HarperCollins Children's, who conceived this project and brought the opportunity to me. She saw where it needed to go and made it happen. Thank you doesn't begin to cover it. You changed my life for the better.

I couldn't have written this without Rebecca Faith Heyman, who edited every word of this book with the valuable combination of patience, speed, and talent. I'm beyond grateful she came on board this project. I'd also like to thank my agent, Carrie Howland, who has been a wonderful resource and team member through the whole process. I'm so grateful for all of her support. I'd also like to thank the remarkable Anna